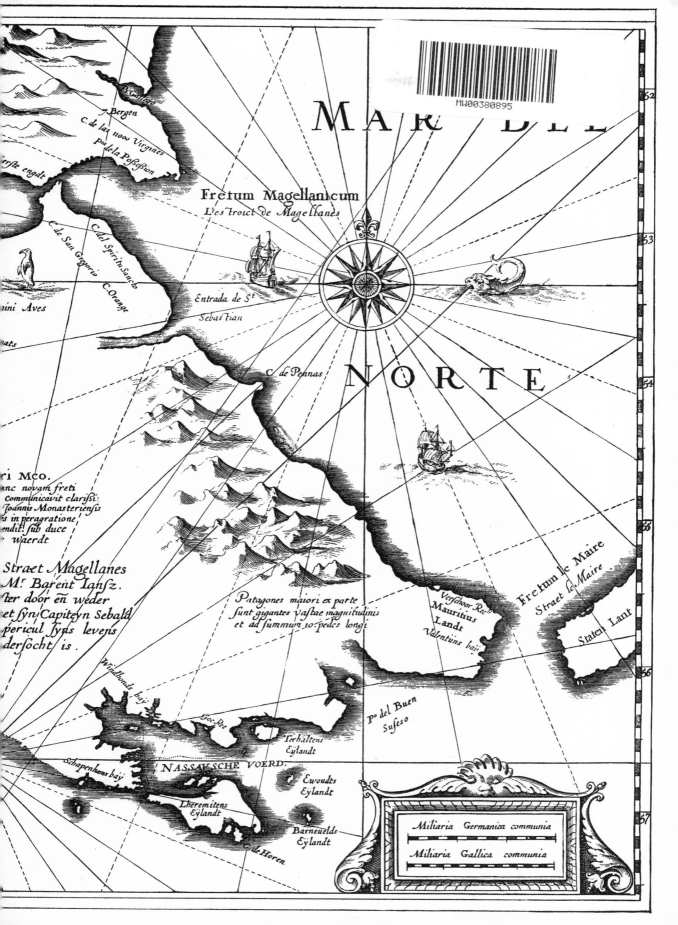

Voyaging

Portrait of me
(improvise)
Rockwell Kent 1923.

Voyaging

SOUTHWARD FROM THE
STRAIT OF MAGELLAN

by

Rockwell Kent

WITH ILLUSTRATIONS BY THE AUTHOR

WESLEYAN UNIVERSITY PRESS
Published by University Press of New England
Hanover and London

Wesleyan University Press
Published by University Press of New England, Hanover, NH 03755

Reprinted by arrangement with the Rockwell Kent Legacies from the 1924 edition published by G. P. Putnam's Sons/The Knickerbocker Press.

Printed in the United States of America

5 4 3 2 1

Seventy-fifth Anniversary Printing, 1999

LIBRARY OF CONGRESS CATALOGING-IN-PUBLICATION DATA

Kent, Rockwell, 1882–1971.
Voyaging southward from the Strait of Magellan / by Rockwell Kent ; with illustrations by the author.
p. cm.
Reprint. Originally published: New York : G.P. Putnam's Sons, 1924.
ISBN 0-8195-6409-5 (pa : alk. paper)
1. Tierra del Fuego (Argentina and Chile)—Description and travel. 2. Magellan, Strait of (Chile and Argentina)—Description and travel. 3. Magallanes y Antârtica Chilena (Chile)—Description and travel. 4. Kent, Rockwell, 1882–1971—Journeys—South America. I. Title.

F2986.K37 2000
918.2'76—dc21

99-48125

To
Kathleen

INTRODUCTION

HERE is a story that treats of a great many bad characters—that is, of those blood-and-thunder fellows who, it is supposed, under pressure of misfortune at home, or natural lawlessness, have fled to the frontier and over, as to the only refuge that would tolerate them. And, as the scene of the story is the worst frontier in the world, its characters are, presumably, the very dregs of humankind, the froth of wickedness. Among them are cannibals, poachers, soldiers, brawlers, missionaries, a governor, a murderer or two, a minister's son, and a Holy-jumper.

Of his own character the author has found it difficult, impossible in fact, to write with honesty. The assumption of incorruptible virtue, by authors of books of travel, has become a fixed tradition, that one who would hold the attention of the virtuous reader would not do well to violate.

And yet, one sensitive to truthfulness may well shrink from such bold-faced effrontery. Therefore have I chosen to cry out my confession in the market place; yet discreetly, in the remote and unfrequented market of the introduction: here, where perchance no curious passer-by will pause to listen, I beat my breast, and, in the best Russian manner, cry out, "Hear ye! hear ye! The 'I' of 'Voyaging,' who through twenty-four chapters parades his virtue, is a myth, a humbug. He is a sinful man."

And in proof of it (for, as a boast of virtue is evidence of wickedness, and of wickedness the contrary, proof is needed), I mind the reader of a discrepancy in Chapter II of the book. There, while our poverty is laid bare, and the hand of others' generosity is displayed as fitting out my mate and me with many things, it is *not* told how and where we got our food supplies for a voyage of many months. *Where* we procured them, since the story of that would involve several persons of high position, will not be told: but *how*, is my confession. We stole them.

We stole them in three separate raids.

On the first raid we netted two hundred pounds of sugar (the owner of this, José Curtze, who later became a close friend of mine, will open his eyes and, I trust, not close his heart at this confession), four hundred pounds of flour, twenty pounds of coffee, ten pounds of tea, twenty-five pounds of beans, six bottles of ketchup, a case of milk, and as much again of things that I've forgotten. The get-away was made in broad daylight.

The second raid was on a dark midnight. We had discovered a cache of stolen table luxuries that some thief had secreted, waiting an opportunity to remove it. "The miserable thief!" we cried; and it gave me some satisfaction to reflect that in this case two wrongs made one unquestionable right. Not stopping to look over our find, we conveyed it in sacks out over the harbor to our boat. What was our pleasure, on arraying it there, to find ourselves possessed of the following: twenty-one jars of sour pickles (domestic and imported), fourteen jars of sweet pickles, eleven jars of strawberry jam, seven jars and two tins of marmalade, thirty-seven tins of fruit, nine tins of black pepper, and seventeen tins of curry powder.

Of the third affair I was at the time a little ashamed. We had already more than we could eat or barter; but our hand was in and we couldn't stop. The loot was a matter of more flour, raisins, prunes, walnuts, etc.—besides two dozen small rockets, ten super rockets, twenty-odd assorted red and blue pilot flares, two dozen bars of lead, and six large bottles of lime juice.

This, if it be understood as merely a suggestion of character, may complete my confession—unless, as a corrective of any misunderstanding of its social side, I mention that after a certain evening's entertainment on the Wollaston Islands I awoke with a memorial gash on the nose.

Those who shall have read the foregoing may wonder, as did my very good and understanding friend, the American Consul at Punta Arenas, why the author is still at large. And yet that is readily explained. Over and above the protection of my own craft and my mate's formidable strength, was the persistent kindness and generosity of those with whom our adventures threw us. And it is with a renewed sense of my gratitude to them that I here subjoin their names:

Captain I. H. Cann, of the S. S. *Curaca*, and officers Reid, Esdon, and Cavaghan, and the ship's carpenter.

Jorge Ihnen, of Punta Arenas.

His excellency V. Fernández, Governor of the Territory of Magallanes, and Austin Brady, and Captain Delaunoy; Señores Sorensen, Willumsen, Curtze, Alonzo, Babut, Holke, Captain Wilson, Captain Grez, and Captain "Jack."

The captain of the *Oneida*, "Lobo del Mar," the donkey engineer of the *Lonsdale*, "Frenchy," and the cook.

Señores Morrison, Marcou, Garese, and Bravo, of Dawson.

Señores Mulach, Lawrence, Lundberg, and Neilsen of Tierra del Fuego; and Antonio, "Curly," Francisco, Christopherson, Nana, and Zarotti.

Vasquez, of the Wollaston Islands.

Captains Dagnino and Acevedo of Talcuhuano.

My brother Eduardo Silva Ruiz of the *Chiloe*.

Captain Neilsen and Mr. Pennington, of the *Taluma*, and Violetta and "Rosa Chileña."

OVER THE ULTIMATE

Who asks when
We that have done with doing and the blood-red tides of men
  Shall hold fast
  Ourselves at last?
Who cares when?

We that have dived o'er the morning and the
    thither sides of night,
What delight?
  Should we have your traces,
  Times and places—
What delight?

Ye that are day-things,
  Reckoners of north and south,
    Of great things ruinous;
    What should ye know of us,
Us that have stars for our playthings,
  Yea, stars that browse on our mouth?

What life saith,
  Shall we care,
We that have juttied through death
  And despair?

We that have joked with the mountain gales
  And sent them rattling home,
We that have held the morning's sails
  O'er the foam?
    Yet laughing at sails and mornings, all things
      that are still or roam?

What life saith
  Of its strife,
  Shall we care?
We that have juttied through death
    And despair,
  Yea, and life!
    Shall we care?
    Of what shall we care?
—BAYARD BOYESEN

CONTENTS

ILLUSTRATIONS

ILLUSTRATIONS

ILLUSTRATIONS

Voyaging

CHAPTER I

WHY AND WHERE

AT last, for the first time in months of fevered work, I paused. The labor, the innumerable difficulties and delays, the anxieties of penury, all, with the launching of my boat from that ship's deck that day, would end. I laughed as I wiped my greasy hands on a piece of waste and tossed it overboard, as I looked down upon the crowd against the rail where my boat hung suspended over the sea. Ancient dismantled hulk, of *your* proud launching had you memories of such a gathering as now appeared upon your deck, of governors and captains, of the rich and cultured and the beautiful? It was spring, there in far southern South America, and the cheeks of the maidens of Punta Arenas glowed with roses such as only the cold, salt sea wind could make bloom. How beautiful appeared the ladies in their brilliant finery upon that dingy, rusted iron deck, with the wide blue water of Magellan's Strait above them! How beautiful the world all glistening in the young September sun, the gleaming white and crimson of the flags whipped in the clean west wind, that wind of youth and gaiety! And on the snow white damask-covered hatch stood crystal glasses and Champagne! Sweet, sweet Champagne! We laughed with happiness; it was the christening of my boat.

We look back upon another spring, mid-spring, and five months earlier in time. It is May in New York. The same west wind has blown the heavens clear; across the profound blue sweep belated clouds trailing their shadows over the city's towers. The sun shines down with such sweet warmth that the stone walls like horns of plenty pour out their living flowers until the pavements are a garden gay and beautiful with life. New York is Paradise in spring, an Eden, with infinitely more of happiness and

(1)

beauty than was ever dreamed of by the shepherd patriarchs. The fruit of happiness and wisdom hangs from boughs so heavy laden down that there's no tempter needed but the fruit itself. There are no gates, no wall, no Cherubim with flaming swords to warn and to expel. Here in this happiness the heart cries out its own despair, speaks its own doom and banishment.

How unobserved and silently is the deep measure of the soul's endurance filled; it mounts the rim, trembles a moment there, then like a torrent overflows—the vast relief of action. This hour you are bound by the whole habit of your life and thought; the next by unerring impulse of the soul you are free. How strong and swift is pride to clear itself, from misery or joy, from crowds, from ease, from failure, from success, from the recurrent brim-full, the too-much! Forever shall man seek the solitudes, and the most utter desolation of the wilderness to achieve through hardship the rebirth of his pride.

Within an hour of the thought that I must go I had secured a clerk's berth on a freighter sailing for the farthest spot on the wild, far southern end of South America, of all lands that one hears or reads of the most afflicted and desolate. Because I loved the cold and desolation and the wilderness? It is hard to say.

Tales of adventure and shipwreck, of month-long battles with the wind and sea to round the Horn, of mountain seas a half a mile between their crests thundering eternally on granite shores, have woven about that region of the Sailor's Graveyard the spirit-stirring glamour of the terrible.

And yet how little is known of that region. The clerk at a book store to whom I applied for a map of Tierra del Fuego looked at me with superior disdain and said he'd never heard of it. No, it is not to landsmen that one should turn for knowledge of the world, for after all their world is but those cluttered portions of the globe that obstruct like reefs the great broad highway of the sea. So in a little store near the water front I found at once what I had sought; and on charts of the sea learned, inversely as it were, and to the precise detail of contour that only mariners' charts possess, what was not sea but land.

And had the spirit of adventure not been stirred by the nomancy of Magellan, Tierra del Fuego and Cape Horn, there in cold print and naked portent appeared such names as Famine Reach, Desolation Bay and Last Hope Inlet; while, suggestive of yet other terrors, stood warnings to shipwrecked mariners against the savage natives of the coast. Here was indubitable confirmation of the glamorous worst that legend had related of that region; and as such it clinched my will to go.

In the confusion, ferment, haste of preparation, three weeks flew by as one; then with paints and canvas, brushes, paper, ink, a tent, blankets, heaps of old clothes and shoes, and a flute—all packed, with seven hundred dollars in my pocket, I was ready. It was the last of May, the eve of sailing. Midnight and pouring rain, the dreary water front heaped high with foreign freight, the pandemonium of harbor sounds

(2)

out of the salt, damp, mystic, fog-enshrouded darkness: there, amid the reek and sound of voyaging, relinquished love and friendship glowed more beautiful than ever.

We sailed. We cleared the Hook, the land dropped down, the hard horizon of the sea encircled us. My life became a memory and the future broke against our prow and shimmered, and was foam and trailed behind us in the steamer's wake. There was no measure of the time but days and nights, and the passage of these was forgotten in the contentment of their monotony, or concealed in the illusion of swiftly changing seasons as from the springtime of the north the steamer bore us southward through six weeks and seven thousand miles, through the mid-summer of the equator to the July winter of the Strait of Magellan.

With the disappearance of land the ship at sea becomes a planetary body moving in the orbit of its prescribed course through the fluid universe of the ocean. It has cast off from the whole accumulated "realities" of life, and these endure but in the memories of the men aboard. Activity is constrained, and the mind turns to contemplation or to thought: the true record of a voyage on the sea must be a record of those illusive imaginings of the almost unconscious mind responding to the hypnotic monotony of the ship's vibrations, of the liquid rustling of the water streaming past her sides, of the endlessly recurrent rhythm of the bow wave, and the even, seething pattern of the wake. The memory of it is of prolonged and changeless contentment.

Of the friendships that by time and circumstances and the dominating monotony of environment were privileged to become close, of those close friendships which also are a part of that intangible but very living intensive experience of the voyage, these pages of dilative adventure may bear no record save the tribute of gratitude that I here pay to Captain Cann of Nova Scotia and to the chief officer, Mr. Reid, of piratical Penzance. But of the third officer with whom less, perhaps, a friendship than a close partnership in adventure came to be shared much must at once be said. And yet, whereas I write of him with the generous permission to handle his life and character with entire frankness, I find myself in turning to his origin and early years confronted with a veil of secrecy that, less—it seemed to me—out of reserve than shame, he never in our eight months of companionship permitted himself to withdraw.

Ole Ytterock was born in Trondhjem, Norway. At fourteen he went to sea on a sailing ship under his father. That father appears to have been a skipper of the grand old school who, having risen through hardship, proposed by hardship to make a man of Ole. After standing a few months of beating the boy deserted in some foreign port. His father dying a few years later, Ole never saw him again. And, having cursed him at parting, he loathed his memory.

For years after that Ole's life was marked by similar adventure. The order and number of his desertions, the catalogue of the foreign seaports with which the debaucheries of his stolen freedom made him familiar, have escaped my memory.

(3)

Twice he deserted in Borneo, only to be recaptured. It must have been in this period of his life that, consequent, I conjecture, upon a return to Norway, he became involved in some disgrace that made him, at least in his own bitterness of mind, a man without a country.

Having deserted in Sydney, Australia, he shipped on a freighter bound for Guayaquil. The crew and officers, with the exception of two men, were blacks, and Ole was unmercifully handled on the trip. He promptly deserted on arrival, and, being now at the age of twenty, enlisted with the rebels of an Equadorian revolution, being given the rank of lieutenant. During a street encounter of the war he was struck on the mouth with an iron bar which knocked out most of his teeth. After a few months he succumbed to typhoid and was confined to the military hospital at Guayaquil. On reaching convalescence he escaped from the hospital, and, in company with another renegade, made his way down the Guayaquil River on a raft, enduring terrific hardships through starvation and heat. They proceeded on foot, barefoot in the hot sands, along the coast for several hundred miles to Callao. There, befriended by the British consul, he obtained a passage to Europe.

Having meantime advanced in his studies of navigation he qualified as chief officer and served in that capacity, to the conclusion of the war, on three successively ill-fated Norwegian steamers. A torpedo fragment, incident to one of the sinkings, further added to the disfigurement of his face. Following this he served for some time—until her loss, I believe—as mate of an American four-masted schooner. Being stranded in New York he entered into negotiation with a firm of lifeboat manufacturers to sail one of their craft single-handed around the world; but through his own demonstration of recklessness he lost their confidence and it fell through. These, with rough accuracy, are the events of the life of Ole Ytterock until I met him, aged twenty-six, as third officer of the S. S. *Curaca*.

He stood five feet eight inches in height, weighed one hundred and fifty-six pounds, and measured forty-two inches about the naked chest. He had a mass of thick black hair low on his forehead, narrow blue eyes and a mouth that was brutally ugly in its disfigurement. But, hard-featured as he was, his face appeared at times quite beautiful with tender kindness of expression.

On the night of my arrival aboard the ship Ytterock was the officer on duty. "He's crazy!" had been his comment when someone informed him of my destination and purpose. Three days later, at his own suggestion, we had become partners in the enterprise.

"But I have no money to pay you," I said.

"I wouldn't let you pay me," he answered.

And so with heads together we pored over the charts, and, discussing every impossibility of adventure, hit upon a plan that was both practicable and alluring: We'd get a lifeboat, deck it and rig it with a mast and sail, and laying our course from the

Strait of Magellan through the mountain-islanded channels west and south of Tierra del Fuego sail around the Horn. Therein lay the chance of getting wrecked or drowned or eaten—and we called it settled.

It was a night of mid-July when we entered the Strait of Magellan, and the dark, low shore of the land was scarcely to be discerned. And it was night, and most of us were sleeping, when with the turning tide we swept through the First and Second Narrows and entered Broad Reach. We woke at the clatter of the winch: it was morning, a blue morning and a clear one with a howling wind. We lay at anchor in the open road of Punta Arenas.

You wonder when you see that harbor first, wonder what miracle of time has carried you back over fifty years to open your eyes upon past glories of the sea. You look—and doubt your senses: there they are, the ships, the barks. What world is this, what port? And then your staring eyes discern the vessels shorn and stripped, with lowered yards, dismasted—hulks.

Beyond them is the city, crowded close—a port of commerce; warehouses, a foundry, shipyards, blocks of office buildings, churches, streets of one-story homes and little shops—there at a mile away one eyeful on the wide, desolate, fire-scarred plain of the continent.

Gasping to breathe we stood there in the gale, my mate and I, and strained to see. Blue, golden day, wild day, exuberant, young. Swiftly and deep the thought of everything had touched us—here on the threshold. Adventurers, alone in a new land, conquerors without a sword, voyagers without a ship, vast needs and little cash, and friendless. With one impulse we turned and saw through eyes that the wind had brought to tears the wild exulting of each other's hearts.

The two days that the *Curaca* lay in Punta Arenas harbor remain in my mind as a prolonged festival, the festival at once of leave-taking and of welcome in a new land. And yet the emotions of leave-taking were uppermost, for in the long voyage the ship had become as home, and the friends aboard as kindred. And in the dark night of parting a poignant forsakenness obliterated the thrill of adventure. Ah God! that wild black night upon the harbor, the confusion, hubbub, turmoil on the ship; the drunken toasts, farewells, that turmoil of the heart, that sublimation of the heart's pain into happiness and of that happiness almost to tears. They're heaving up: "On board the tug!—Farewell!" We drop away, the widening black water tosses up the ship's reflected lights like flames. We pass out of the illuminated radius into the darkness, and by the darkness into the solitude of the world's end.

CHAPTER II

SAIL OR JAIL

A WEEK had passed: the friendliness of Chile had enfolded us. It proved no
little thing to have been sponsored in Punta Arenas by the most popular
captain on the coast, and the embarrassment and anxiety of appearing
among strangers in the rôle of mad adventurer was promptly alleviated
by the frank good will and unequalled generosity that was accorded us. To our needs
the most important individual of the territory was Jorge Ihnen, the maritime manager of the largest shipping interests of the port. He was a young man of distinguished
presence, endowed with a humanly penetrating understanding, warm sympathy and
imagination. His decisions about character were made at a glance, and his approval
was backed by sustained confidence and active support. During my first conversation
with him he subjected me to close but not unfriendly scrutiny. At last he said
magnificently:

"If there is anything at any time that you want, come to me and ask for it."

There proved to be very little that at some time I didn't want, but nothing, great
or small, that was not granted. And if, with due modesty, I attribute our sailing
southward at last in a well equipped boat of our own in some degree to our own
persistent labor, it was due vastly more to the friendship of Ihnen and those whom
through him we came to know. On the very day of our arrival a boat was found for
us, and with that at once our greatest care was gone.

And that week later as I sat with my mate in the snug, floating quarters that had
become our home and talked of our windfall of good fortune it seemed suddenly to us
poor four-flushing adventurers, that we were as the King and Duke in "Huckleberry
Finn," and that if our prosperity increased an enraged populace must some day turn

(6)

and drive us out of town. But as the weeks went on and we continued undetected, honored, we, like other impostors, came to believe in ourselves as King and Duke by the grace of God. And of what our life had become, here is the picture:

It is night, in the harbor of Punta Arenas. The hulk of the old ship *Lonsdale* swings gently rocking at her moorings. In the mahogany furnished cabin of the captain, long untenanted, sleep we two. The morning comes, we wake in darkness, light the lamp and dress. I grope my way up the companionway into the piercing cold. Some snow has fallen and my steps sound muffled on the iron deck. Over the black water a golden streak of dawn breaks through low-hanging clouds. Masthead lights gleam over the shadowy forms of ships, and from the city glitter the lamps of early risers. It is profoundly still. I draw a pail of icy water from the tank and wash, and, shivering, dive down below. In the old ship's saloon a swinging lamp burns feebly losing its light upon the dust-grey floor and ceiling and in the shadowy confusion of the sails and ship's gear littering the walls and corners. The pot-bellied iron stove glows red. My mate has finished sweeping, and as the dust cloud settles down we move a little table to the heat. The cook comes in with coffee. Good. Here sit we two amid the early-morning dark and cold of a Magellan winter toasting our legs and ribs at the hot fire and warming our bellies with the boiling drink.

The bump and rubbing of a heavy boat along our ship, the clattering of wooden ladder steps against the iron sides, voices of men, the tramp of heavy boots on deck: these tell that it is seven and the working-day has begun. On the forward deck two carpenters report to me for work.

Against the starboard rail, blocked up and braced to stay upright, was the boat that I had bought, a lifeboat from the wrecked steamer *Beacon Grange*. The boat's length was twenty-six feet, her beam eight feet six, her depth inside three feet and an inch or two. She was a double-ender, clinker built, with light, bent ribs. The stem was splintered, seven planks were stove or rotten; she was warped, dry as a bone and open everywhere. She was of slipshod factory construction with every knee and brace a false one sawed from straight-grained plank. Such was our boat, a derelict. She cost me twenty dollars.

From then onward—every waking hour, week days, Sundays, feast days, dawn till bedtime, in sun or rain or snow or wind we worked upon that boat. We shaped a curved, gnarled root into a stern; we fitted new planks to the damaged sides; we gave her a strong, deep, hardwood keel and shod it with heavy iron; we warped timbers for the deck and cabin. From that turmoil of activity resounded the din of a shipyard: the blows of the hammer and the tap, tap, tap on the rivets, the song of the saw, the thunderclaps of falling planks, the clangorous beating of iron at the forge, the hiss of the torch, the raucous tearing of the scraper over nails and sand. Thus—in snow and sleet and drenching rain and winter cold, with numb hands and icy feet, with laughter and song—these were the sound of us, the breath of us, the life of us for days that became weeks, and weeks that made a month—and two; and still we worked.

We lived aboard our hulks like kings, we tasted mutton seven different ways a day, our beds to tired bodies were as soft as dream clouds; yet—that old *Lonsdale* was a madhouse. She was a sepulchre of derelicts, of men still living on in futile hope—or none, with life behind them.

There were four men besides us two aboard the ship. They occupied what had once been the officers' quarters aft of the saloon. They messed by themselves and at night kept closely to their rooms—except one, an old Frenchman, who was constantly with us in the long evenings. Frenchy was a good-hearted sober man; the others as their moods permitted them were generous and friendly or morosely indifferent. They were failures, sunk through inaction into sterile intentioning or mutton-witted complacency.

There was little drinking on the ship, but occasionally there were orgies that enlivened an entire week. One night is a fair picture of such holidays.

Crash. A roar of curses. Crash, a heavy weight falls on the floor. The tinkle of broken glass. Silence.—— Suddenly a door is hurled open and back against a wooden wall. Heavy footsteps cross the passage and enter another room. Voices, the scuffling of chairs, a roar and then a savage laugh—and Frenchy pops in to us his round and rosy face staring with the fright of some poor little hunted creature. He doesn't speak; but, getting a pack of cards from a shelf, draws a long bench close to the light and us, straddles it, and feverishly lays out the cards for solitaire. There is a moment's peace; then a great bulk of something stirs and lurches down the passage towards us, muttering ominously. A huge form fills the doorway, a rhinoceros of a Norwegian, coarse and heavy-featured with round watery blue eyes, red lids and puffy sockets. He gives a hitch to his pants and like a rolling ship comes in. "Good evening, gentlemen," he says with impertinent obsequiousness, and drops upon the bench. Frenchy has fled.

He talks with the incoherence of a maudlin drunkard; and, after a preamble, says this with some distinctness: "Misher Kent or cap'n or king, whatever you are, I'm drunk, anoiam."

While he gathers his wits to continue, his fingers work as if they played a piano. "What I was gonersay," he gets out with sudden explosive effrontery and a terrific effort at concentration. "We don't like Americans on this ship—get me? An' there's goner be some shootin'."

To avoid trouble, I am trying, during this, to keep my mind upon a very delicate drawing upon which I am busied. I don't look up. He continues.

"I'm the strongest man on this ship, I'm the strongest man in the territory, an' I can throw——"

My mate by this is on his feet:

(8)

THE *LONSDALE*

"Stand up, you miserable white-livered pot-bellied bluff, stand up and I'll sit you on your ear so dam quick——"

"Could you do that to me?" queries the big fellow quite piteously.

"You bet your damned life I could," roars my furious mate.

"Well," says the mighty one ever ever so gently, "maybe you could." And, as if suddenly become very old and tired, he gets laboriously up from his seat and leaves us.

Meanwhile as the weeks flew by, and the boat forever neared but never reached completion, another worry than that of elapsing time arose: approaching penury. Despite the fact that we had lived board free on the *Lonsdale*, there were the wages of the men to be paid every Saturday night and the constant retail purchase to be met of such supplies as were needed in the reconstruction of the boat. There were expenses incidental to our visits ashore—to which the mate's periodical debauches, until I checked them, contributed not a little—and to which the famed conviviality of Punta Arenas contributed a great deal. "It is the general rule with the inhabitants of the 'Campo'," wrote Captain Bové of the Italian Royal Navy, in 1884, "that whatever one takes into the so-called colony (Punta Arenas) must all be left behind; to go away from it with a farthing would be so infamous as to cut off the delinquent from all human fellowship." And for the avoidance of such infamy Punta Arenas is blessedly supplied with tabernacles.

Well, we had been two months in Punta Arenas and—but for a little sum that I had saved to meet an impending enormous bill for wire, cordage, canvas, chains, paint, foundry work and what not, and put aside for presents for the kind fellows on the *Lonsdale* who had helped us—I was penniless. Yet had I known in what good hands we were it would have caused me less concern than it did. One reckless night at the Magellan Club illuminated me. After several rounds of drinks amongst a party of six the checks had all fallen to the lot of one man, except a check for forty cents that was mine.

"I'll throw you for that and pay them all," said he.

"Done," said I, and I threw—and lost.

"Again."—I lost.

Within two minutes the whole pile, amounting to the huge sum of eight American dollars, lay before me. Fortunately I *could* pay it, and I called the attendant. Suddenly the man on my left reached over and swept the whole pile away from me, at the same time instructing the attendant to refuse my money.

"No," they said, "you're our guest in Punta Arenas and you're not allowed to pay."

Nevertheless that great bill for supplies hung over me like the sword of Damocles. Though I had already asked for it the compilation of so compendious a document appeared to demand innumerable consultations between the heads of departments. "Sail or jail," I muttered as I went about. One day I was called into the office of Captain Delaunoy, the port captain, and Mr. Sorensen, the fleet engineer.

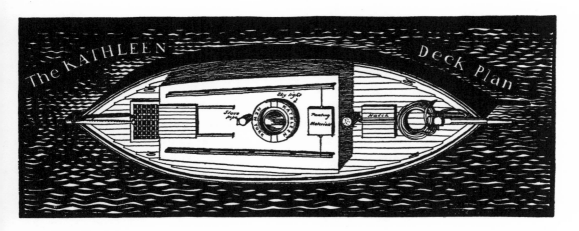

"This item of paint," they questioned me, "you used that on work for us, didn't you? And these pine boards?"

"No," I said, "they were for me."

I went into Ihnen's office. "I want the bill," I said.

He finished what he was doing, rose from his desk and came to the window.

"What's the matter?" he asked putting his hand on my shoulder and turning my face to the light.

I felt as if tears were coming to my eyes. "Nothing," I answered.

Ihnen smiled. He rang for his secretary and dispatched him with a message to Captain Delaunoy. In a few minutes the secretary returned and the bill was handed to me.

"Three—four—five thousand pesos," I cried to myself to steel my courage against the bill's pronouncement of my bankruptcy.

I opened it. It was a short document of about a dozen items: the boat, a little paint, some rope, some odds and ends: the total—I've forgotten; it was nothing.

Ihnen was again busy writing. He was not to be thanked—till now.

And there is another incident that I may here relate that it may not appear that the *Latin* American heart is the only kind one. Mr. Brady, the American consul in Punta Arenas, had from the beginning been a staunch friend to our crack-brained enterprise and to us.

"Come," he said to me, that momentous day before at last we sailed, "we're going shopping. What do you want?"

"Onions," I said—and he bought them.

"Baking powder—cheese—an alarm clock." These and more were purchased—besides a bottle of his pet specific for the "grippe" that I appeared to be ailing with.

Then returning to the Consulate he presented me with an American flag and a large envelope that he said contained my sailing orders—"not to be opened until at sea."

I opened them at sea. The envelope contained two hundred and fifty pesos. "Sail as you please," I read them.

But to return: The boat now lacked nothing but a few last touches of luxury and art, and these a week at most would see supplied. She was decked and cabined, caulked and painted and varnished. The spars had been my work. From sound and straight Norwegian spruce I'd planed and tapered them and scraped and polished them. To the least detail they were beautifully done. My mate meanwhile had made the sails; they were of heavy duck, and strong enough, as I said prophetically at that time, to tear the boat itself apart. Sailmaker and rigger, you'd look far for a better one than the mate. However, with only a few last touches to add, a bit of caulking, a seam to putty, last dabs of paint or varnish, last touches everywhere of no necessity but of vast importance to us, that last week before the launching was whirlwind climax to long weeks of effort. Far into the nights we worked with lanterns on the deck or tween-decks where the spars and rigging were assembled. But always, however time might press, we held to a high standard, slighting nothing. And in my delight with the perfection of the boat I likened it to the one-horse shay. It shall be all, I proudly thought, so evenly and sufficiently strong, from the shoe of the keel to the eye of the peak flag-halyards, that nothing can go wrong with her until the end of time.

This was to be the farthest south launching in all history of an American ship, and we determined to do it magnificently making the occasion an imposing example of Yankee efficiency. All kinds of help was given us. They sent a gang aboard to clean the hulk and to remove the litter and left-over material of our work. The deck was made beautifully tidy. The derrick tackles were inspected, blocks were oiled, new rope was sent aboard for slings.

It is the day before the launching, steam is in the winch, our boat stands in the slings. We're flying about adding the last touches of perfection to order already more than good enough. Yet that last day is far too short. It is late, very late at night, when I bring out from concealment an empty champagne bottle, carry it quietly on deck and fill it with the amber water from the tank. Taking it down again into my cabin I whittle a mushroom stopper for its top out of cork from an old life belt. This I wire carefully and tight so that the cork bulges out between the crossings of the wire. Then I coat the top above the label with glue and, producing a piece of tin foil saved from cigarettes, clap it on, rubbing it so that it adheres tightly. When I have dusted off the loose tin foil, rubbed it a bit, and dusted on some dirt from the floor, I have what appears to be a virgin bottle of Champagne. It is for the christening.— This more than anything declares our penury.

The Great Day opens up its eyes so bright and beautiful that it might be God's

KATHLEEN AS SHE WAS

birthday-blessing on our little boat. Breathless with haste and the confusion of last-minute needs we feel the hours slip by like moments. Suddenly in the midst of things a steamer blows, and the harbor tug, brilliant with flags aloft and a gay crowd on deck, bears down. The hour is at hand.

And now in that hour we have reached the moment with which this story began. Governors and captains, a consul, editors, sweet women and pretty girls are crowded about the launching platform. It was a moment to pause; and if as a tumult of thought sped through my mind I mechanically wipe the dirt of labor from my hands upon a piece of waste, and throw the waste into the sea, it is at once the unconscious gesture of completed toil and a symbol of the restored serenity of a distraught adventurer's mind. The christening is at hand. There where the infant boat hangs at the rail's side in the slings stands a beautiful Chilean girl with my poor Champagne bottle, gaily draped with bunting, in her hand. She speaks:

"Le nombro Catalina, barquito nuestro, que te acompañe la benedición de Dios en tu viaje."

She breaks the bottle; and the amber fluid flows like rarest wine over the bows. At that instant the *Kathleen* with the mate standing proudly on board dropped smoothly down and kissed the sea.

"Mother," a little girl was saying as the bottle broke, "it splashed in my face."

"Never mind, dear," answered her sweet mother, "it was good Champagne."

The last days are upon us. I get our sailing dispatch from the Captain of the port, and mark our probable course on the chart.

"If you're not back in four months," he says, "we'll send a cruiser to find you."

I make my will at the Consulate, receive the Godspeed of the Governor, the Godspeed of our friends—and the eventful morning dawns.

The last honors of a departing ship are accorded us. Towed by the harbor-launch, toasted and cheered by friends aboard, we pass out through the shipping and cast off. And as the wind lays us over and we bear away, we roar across the widening water the old sailing ship chantey, "Rolling Home." And though the words we made for it are not poetry I give them here, since to us and to those who that day heard them they spoke the thrill of our adventure.

> So farewell to Punta Arenas
>   And its maidens bright and fair;
> Though the cannibals should eat us,
>   Still our hearts lie buried there.
>
> *Chorus.* Rolling home, etc.

VOYAGING

Though the Cape Horn swell engulf us,
  And the ocean be our grave,
There'll be many there to greet us
  In the "graveyard" of the brave.

Chorus. Rolling home, etc.

And many verses more—long after none but ourselves and the west wind heard the sound of them. And as Punta Arenas faded from our view we still could see the red, white and blue of Chile dipping in salute to us from the masthead of the *Lonsdale*.

CHAPTER III

SAIL!

DOWN the long stretch of Broad and Famine Reach stand the white peaks and ranges of the wilderness, with all the threat and promise of their mysteries: and still beyond and high above them all the unattainable white peaks of Sarmiento. Ah, what a day! So sharp and blue, and golden where the far sky touches the circle of the world! The lower atmosphere is glistening with the spray of wind-blown wave crests. A double rainbow spans the west, an omen of strong wind and of good fortune; and, where it rests among the mountains of the south, there in some peaceful, solitary virgin valley, lies the forever sought and undiscovered gold of happiness.

With sails all set and drawing full the little *Kathleen*, wind abeam, lies over on her side and with the main boom trailing in the water and the deck awash goes like a wild thing fled to freedom. "Don't ease her!" cries the mate. Her bows shiver the seas, the cold spray wets us. A school of porpoises is racing, leaping, plunging round us. Good luck! The gods are with us!

The wind has risen and the seas run high. Great crested waves bear down and threaten us—and laugh, and lift us tenderly, and cradle us. We *ride* the seas. Our ship is tight and strong; she sails, and holds her course unswervingly. "A beauty!" cries the mate; and with my soul on eagle-wings of happiness I go below.

There in the cabin was the final word of cleanliness and order. There were convenient shelves with tins of food set out in orderly array, with pots and dishes in their place secured against the tossing of the boat, with space for linen and for books and cameras and paints; there were the racks for instruments and charts, for the compass and the clock and the lamp, and for pens and brushes, for saws and hammers and

(16)

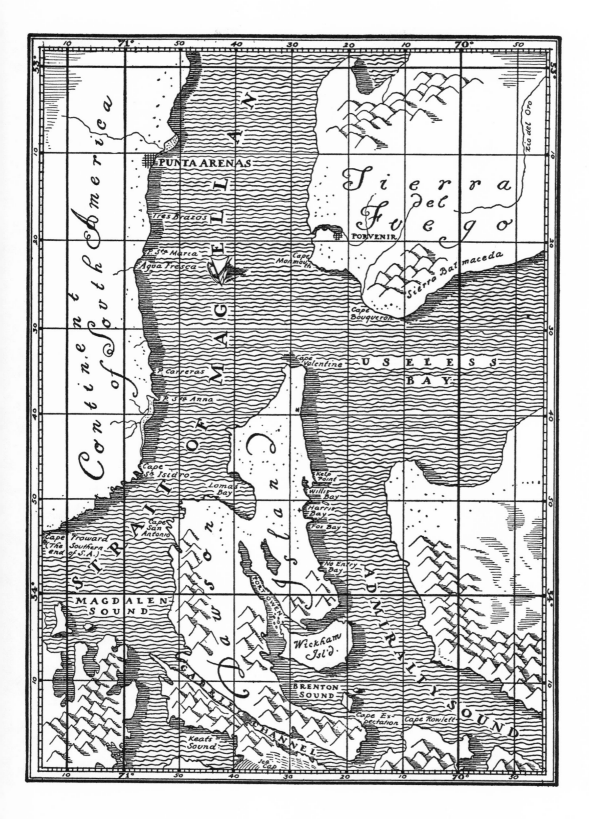

pliers and files, for the marlinspike and the caulking iron, for the lead line, for the flags and pilot lights and rockets, for my canvases and paper. Our beds were cleverly contrived: on canvas, laced across, we had spread our store of clothes and made a mattress of them. The beds were laid this day all clean and sweet for night. The stove was polished and the floor was scrubbed. It was perfection in that little cabin—all but a cup or so of water that had leaked up from the bilge and slopped around untidily in a corner of the floor.

I took a cup to bail it out, chatting meanwhile through the open companionway with the mate.

"With the wind holding like this," he said as a fresh squall struck and heeled us over, "we should get to Willis Bay by five o'clock this afternoon." It was now about eleven, and in an hour and a half we had covered perhaps twelve miles. Our course was for Cape Valentine on Dawson Island. In two days, we figured it, we'd reach the head of Admiralty Sound; in two days more be out and headed westward to round the point of Brecknock Peninsula.

And all the time I bailed.

Quite innocent of trouble it occurred to me that one might have done it better with a kettle than a cup. I take a kettle, plant one foot upon the boat's sloping side to brace myself, and set to work in earnest.

The mate is singing as the spray flies over him. His is a happiness too great to bear alone. He is in love and she is many thousand miles away. A kettle of cold water on his legs startles him out of it.

A quarter of an hour has passed. I'm bailing desperately, emptying the water over the mate, his tender heart and everything. I'm standing in it to my knees, and steadily it rises. There's not one chance of beating back to the near windward shore; we change our course to run to leeward fifteen miles away. There's a gale and a high sea, and our boat is sodden with the weight of water in her. In turns we bail, work to exhaustion, both of us; and steadily, from God knows where, she fills.

And then the truth strikes home—we're sinking. And the land's too far away to reach.

We come about to lower sail. The gaff jambs, and the mate scrambles aloft to trample on it. In a fury of beating and slatting and the clattering of blocks and whipping of the halyards down it comes—and we lie hove-to under the staysail.

The skiff that we carry on the deck is eight feet long, four wide, flat-bottomed; it's of no conceivable use in a sea. Nevertheless we launch it and make it fast astern, and while it bucks like an enraged animal to dislodge me, I succeed with canvas and tacks in decking it over. I stow oars and life belts and a few necessities on board, stick my opened clasp knife in the bow to cut us free at the last moment from the wreck, and the lifeboat is ready.

Seen from the skiff, the forlorn condition of the *Kathleen* was apparent. She lay there listing heavily, with half the deck submerged; and every sea broke over her. Suddenly I was overwhelmed by the hopelessness of the conviction of catastrophe. There was neither thought of God nor fear of death but only a poignant vision of my life as finished and left pitifully incomplete, a lightning-flash of home with the little children and their mother weeping there, a sickening shame at death so futile and so miserable as this, an instant of vertigo, a weakening of the knees, a griping of the bowels as though I hung over an immense and sheer abyss, a wild impulse to madness —to throw my arms aloft and scream. Then swiftly, at the very breaking point of all control, profounder shame swept that whole agony aside and left the mind unburdened of all memory. So that with humor I could listen to the mate's wild strong young voice sing "Smile a while," to the swashing rhythm of his bailing; and I could note the little quaver in it, and, understanding song and quaver, laugh to think that even he got just a little touched by fear.

We stood in the cabin almost to our waists in water, and bailed in turns. The place was devastated. With the rolling of the boat the water swashed about and swept our treasures from the shelves. Shoes, socks, linen, paper, bread, cocoa, curry powder, nuts and cigarettes covered the tide and swirled about the vortex of the pail. My bunk was flooded so that the blankets floated out.

I took the log book of the *Kathleen*, sat down on the edge of the bunk, and on the clean first page wrote this, "our epitaph," I thought.

"First day out, three hours from sailing. Boat half full of water, hove-to. Bailing in turns. Lifeboat equipped to cross to Porvenir. Strong west wind blowing. Mate singing, great fellow. No chance to save anything; lifeboat is too small."

Then, tying up a few treasures in a waterproof package, I was ready.

That the *Kathleen* would sink was inevitable. For an hour we had fought against the water; we had done our best and were incapable of greater effort, and we had never for a moment checked the water's rise. The end was not a matter of guess but of exact calculation. I *knew* that in ten minutes more the ship would sink. Intelligence excluded hope.

My mate was gifted with many noble and endearing qualities: he was courageous, good-natured and doggedly perseverant. But of intelligence—the power to reason, to deduce effect from cause—he had absolutely none. And it was pathetic, not only to observe him in the face of the tragically apparent futility of all that we could do stubbornly plying the heavy pail to the everlasting rhythm of his song, but to reflect that in his blindness to the imminence of death he missed the glory and the pain of life's high moment. He was too dull to know that we were doomed!

So we bailed and sang. Five minutes went, and ten. We passed the limit of the time that reason had allowed the boat to live; yet still she floated, rolling sluggishly. And as the seas piled over her there seemed each time no chance that she'd emerge again. Time brought new energy. We fought the water stubbornly.

(20)

FAIR WIND

Not daring to hope, we bailed—for it was all that there was left in life to do. The *Kathleen* didn't sink.

Days later when we beached her we understood the cause of her misfortune and salvation. That day her floating was a miracle. Slowly it dawned upon us as we worked that we had stopped the water's rise; and when at last we knew beyond all doubt that we could hold our own it was, strangely, without emotion that we received our lives again.

It was by now perhaps two in the afternoon. The water in the cabin was still up to our knees, and it required continuous bailing to hold it. Ruined supplies of every kind floated about, and our fair ship, four hours ago so trim and beautiful, was now the picture of desolation. The wind and sea abated as the day wore on; we took so little water now that by our bailing every minute showed it lower; and presently, with not a foot's depth left, we hoisted a reefed mainsail, came about, and started on a long tack for the windward shore some miles away.

The afternoon increased in beauty and in peacefulness; and as the certainty of our

(21)

security became established, profound contentment arose like the morning sun within us. Life is so infinitely sweet and rich that nothing matters—only that we live.

Evening comes on, the shadows of the land creep out across the sea and cover us. It's cold. On the last breath of the dying wind we reach our anchorage.

How still it is! Darkness has almost hidden the abandoned whaling village on the shore. Dimly the forms of stores and houses detach themselves from the dark ground. In one house burns a lamp. A man is driving cattle down the silent street. Treeless sand hills enclose the little plain on which the settlement is built; beyond them stands the barrier of snow-topped mountains. . . . For long minutes we have not spoken.

We go below. There's a damp fire burning and it's faintly warm. We are dead tired. Wrapping ourselves in soaking blankets we lie down in wet beds to sleep.

CHAPTER IV

JAIL?

THAT first long miserable night the hours seemed years. An east wind raised a swell that bore in from the open strait and rocked our little vessel at her anchorage. Shivering and tossing in our soaking beds, sleeping a little while from sheer exhaustion to wake as cold as ice, churning our legs for warmth, beating our arms, dawn came at last, and in its smile all memory of our misery vanished. The calm of that new sunrise and the clean sweet morning air were drafts of courage. Deep we drank. Again far off across the blue and peaceful strait glistened the snowy mountains of the wilderness, commanding us. Heave up the anchor, voyagers! Heave away! Heave! We drew the anchor dripping on the deck. The gentle west wind filled the sail; she heeled; the water rippled past her side. Southward again we bore away.

Southward, but timidly. With reefed mainsail we skirted the shore, watching the water in the bilge as one would hold a fevered pulse and count its beats. She leaked —a very little; and as the wind held moderate, our confidence returned. We left the shore, and laid our course by chart to cross the strait and make Cape Valentine, the northern point of Dawson Island.

Meanwhile one man worked to restore a semblance of order to the cabin. Appearance has at times a grateful eloquence and affects the mind more forcibly than the reality; and there is a sure relief from the distress of misfortune to be found in prettily concealing it from sight. We hid our drenched and ruined property, wrung out our soaking clothes and blankets, packed them in sacks, and stowed them in the forward hold. To the damage that had been done to the bulk of our supplies in both our main storage spaces, forward and aft, we that day shut our eyes, though it was not long before the stench of moldering food drove us to thoroughness.

(23)

CAPE VALENTINE

We cleaned the rusted stove, and polished it, and lit a cheering fire. We cooked good food, and ate, and were content. And although as the day advanced the wind increased, so that the water entered and kept us bailing, no near danger threatened; and our thoughts could trifle with the dread of what might come, and only savor our contentment.

Only the voyager perceives the poignant loveliness of life, for he alone has tasted of its contrasts. He has experienced the immense and wild expansion of the spirit outward bound, and the contracted heartburn of the homecoming. He has explored the two infinities—the external universe—and himself.

Only the voyager discovers—and by discovery he generates. For of man's universe, which is but that portion of the infinite which he perceives, he is, by his perception of it, the creator. Thus in his own image has man created God.

The wilderness is kindled into life by man's beholding of it; he is its consciousness, his coming is its dawn. Surely the passion of his first discovery carries the warmth and the caress of a first sunrise on the chaos of creation.

So, like a sun, we climbed the hilltop of the sea and with the thrill of wonder saw new lands unfold themselves. The long shore of Dawson Island was before us, a treeless waste of sand cliffs, cloud-shadowed, desolate and wind-swept. And the dark sea broke in gleaming surf along the beach. And although with the nearing of the land the strait was safely crossed, our relief was tempered by the frown of the unfriendly coast we'd made.

Off Cape Valentine is a long reef with outlying shoals and fields of kelp. We gave these dangers a wide berth, passed them, and entered the calm water of the island's lee. And almost at that moment the sun broke through the clouds; it cheered and warmed us. Its golden light transfused the scene and threw a new enchantment over everything.

The low sun's shadows raised into relief the strangely channeled sand cliffs of the coast and made the vari-colored clumps of bushes show like jewels, dark and glistening, on the yellow fields and bogs. Clefts in the shore revealed the inland plain and forests of tall green-leafed trees with somber-shadowed depths. Eastward lay the seemingly limitless expanse of Useless Bay; and straight before us, far beyond the horizon of the sound, ranges of snow white peaks closed in the south.

Darkness came on when we were miles from port, and only deeper blackness showed the contour of the land against the sky. A strong east wind had risen, and in the glamour of the night and the wild noises of the wind and sea we seemed to drive on with unearthly speed.

On Offing Island, off the mouth of Willis Bay, was a light we steered by, though its dazzling flashes only deepened the obscurity about us. The mate, from his lookout forward, at last made out the black mass of the point of land we had to turn. We drove nearer, keeping it a few points off the starboard bow; we were rounding it.

What happened to the mate's wits for a moment I don't know. But suddenly he screamed out, "Keep her off!" I did. And we shot through the churned white water of a reef we'd missed by not our length.

Within the bay where the calmer water reflected the black shadow of the land was darkness that no eyes could penetrate. Sounding continually we searched the shores for the narrow entrance of a sheltered cove that we'd been told of, but the deceptive contours of the forest hid it from us; and finding ourselves at last at the head of the bay, in shoal water among reefs and flats, we dropped anchor in two fathoms.

While the mate put the deck in order I rowed out in the skiff to explore the surroundings of our anchorage. All around were shoals on which we must have grounded had good fortune not favored us.

That night in the security of the wilderness we laid aside the burden of our troubles and, peacefully as little children, slept.

We awoke in a new world, tranquil, sunlit and profoundly silent; and, in the varied splendor of its vegetation, almost tropical. The forest towered over us, tall evergreens with densely intermingling tops, and flowering shrubs and vines and mossy parasites nourished to rank luxuriance by a rain-soaked soil. The calm bay mirrored back a

(25)

OFF DAWSON ISLAND

cloudless sky; and, in the breathlessness of that spring morning, the sun shone on us with a summer's warmth.

We were anchored only a few yards from the narrow entrance of the cove that we'd been looking for the night before. Having explored it in the skiff and found it to be quite perfect for a permanent anchorage and for beaching our boat for examination and repair, we hove anchor and proceeded to tow the *Kathleen* through the channel. Meanwhile, however, the west wind had begun to blow; and before we could enter the cove it gained such force that we were checked, and, in spite of all that we could do by towing with the skiff and sculling with a long sweep on the *Kathleen*, slowly driven back to the mouth of the channel. Here, in the wind and current, we anchored, decidedly worse off for having tried to better our position.

With the saturated condition of everything on board there was immediate work to be done. Soon blankets, sweaters, coats, socks, shirts and drawers flapped like holiday flags from the rigging; and, if a thorough examination of our stores brought home to us the full extent of our loss and damage, there was at least some satisfaction got from throwing the spoiled stuff overboard. The most irreparable loss was of a small kodak. The salt water had rusted the balanced mechanism of the shutter

(26)

beyond repair, and I was reduced to lug about throughout my travels a cumbersome and heavy Graflex.

In style that fitted the exhilaration of our mood we served ourselves afternoon tea. It was warm and cosy in the little cabin, and the purring of the kettle and the gurgle of the tide against the boat's thin sides were apt accompaniment to our contentment. For a long time neither of us spoke.

"Mate," I said at last, "this is our first day in the wilderness; and we have both realized, I think, particularly after the hectic months of getting ready and too many people, what peace is to be found in being alone. And, as the only human beings of the place, we have now tasted the elation of supremacy. It's more than freedom; in a sense we're kings."

At that instant something struck the side of the boat; footsteps sounded on the deck. As we sprang toward the companionway there appeared, glaring at us, the unprepossessing and stupid face of a soldier.

"Ustedes están arrestados," he growled.

We were prisoners.

CHAPTER V

LAID UP

PORT HARRIS, on Dawson Island, is the only settlement in the archipelago west of Tierra del Fuego. Its romantic history dates from forty years or more ago; a period when, incidental to the white man's occupation of the prairie lands of southern Patagonia, there was carried on a ruthless war to exterminate the aborigines. Inhabiting the interior of Tierra del Fuego were the Ona Indians, a superb race related to the giant natives of the mainland north of the Strait of Magellan. Their warring and predatory habits brought them into immediate conflict with the white invaders of their lands. Thefts of the settlers' sheep caused stern measures of retaliation, until the misunderstanding of two alien races, that diplomacy might have converted into friendship, grew into a bloody conflict. Soldiers were sent to garrison the farms; and, as an inducement to ruffians out of employment to join in the good work, a pound a head was offered for dead Indians. The war became a loathsome butchery.

Deeply moved to pity by this revolting carnage, the local diocese of the Silecian order established a mission at Port Harris for the persecuted savages, and undertook with the sincerest Christian intent to instruct them in the graces of civilization, to teach them to labor, and to incline their hearts toward God. So the astonished Indians in many hundreds were, by the soldiers, herded up like sheep and driven on board ships, and bound and dumped like mutton into the hold, and conveyed to Dawson Island.

About that ill-fated missionary enterprise are told stories of the most loathsome debauchery and crime; in the absence of apparent motive they are incredible. It is told and generally believed that on the arrival of the first consignment of natives they

(28)

were received with Judas-like expressions of kindness by the black-hearted priests. They were conducted to a banquet lavishly set out, and there fed poisoned food. They feasted and died. Although on the whole ridiculous, the details of this horrible legend follow closely what actually occurred, as it was told to me by a now unbiased eye-witness of the event. On the arrival of the ship, the Silecian Superior, with the great spirit of the early Catholic missionaries of the north, assuming full responsibility for the conduct of the savages, ordered them unbound and set at liberty. They were then led to a great feast that had been prepared for them. Half starved from their recent captivity, and, moreover, ever unaccustomed to such bounty, they gorged their bellies beyond nature's tolerance. And in the agonies of indigestion many of them died.

Not to meddlers with the lives of others shall one look for understanding. No horrors of experience deterred these Christians from the ruthless pursuit of their benevolence. They fed their wards and clothed and trained them; and when, after a course of years and in spite of a continued replenishment of healthy savages from the wilderness of Tierra del Fuego, the human material had about all died, the mission went the way of bankrupt things; it was put on the block and sold.

Port Harris now became the center of a business enterprise. The first act of the new manager was to set up a keg of beer for the man who should throw a lariat around the cross of the church. Down came the cross amid the hurrahs of the crowd. They built a sawmill and a shipyard; and there on Dawson Island was eventually launched the famous and ill-fated *Sara*, the largest ship ever built in Chile.

It was dark when, escorted by soldiers and towed by their launch, we entered Harris Bay. The electric lights of the little town sparkled through the rigging of vessels at the wharf, and were reflected wavering in the black water. And, if the illusion of our isolation had been shattered by the sudden appearance of belligerent men, we now, having cleared ourselves of a mistaken identity with pirates that had brought them down on us, rejoiced in the good fortune of the port's friendship. The *Kathleen* was to be properly docked and put in order.

The whistle of the mill announced the dawn; and, as its echoes died, the whirr and screaming of the saw, the clatter of the donkey engine, the clamor of falling planks, the shouts of bosses, the wild cursing of bullock drivers, the whole noise of a mill's activity filled the air.

We moved the *Kathleen* to an anchorage abreast of the slip and waited for the tide for docking her. The bright paint on her sides, the varnish of her spars, the polished brass of her fittings, glistened in the sun; and from her masthead waved the stars and stripes. What though in sailing she had almost come to pieces! There was in her appearance such trimness and beauty, and in the flag such huge prestige of power as must, we thought, excite beholders to respect and admiration.

(29)

I was in the cabin, at work.

Suddenly the mate, who had been ashore, burst in, his face crimson with passion. "The carabineros are here," he cried. "They've ordered the flag down. I told them to go to Hell. They want your papers."

Now I am too old an American not to have had the percentage of my patriotism somewhat worn by travel and diluted by reflection; and in my heart I'd dipped the flag a hundred times to other flags that were the symbol of virtues un-American. The Norwegian mate's Americanism was one hundred plus; and so fiercely raged the flames of outraged loyalty as he stood there before me, that I was both impressed and afraid. So, concealing my passport and sailing dispatch in my shirt, and, prudently, leaving him and his ungovernable rage behind, I went ashore.

Two carabineros, splendidly accoutred, stood there. A crowd was gathering. The faces of the soldiers were characteristic of the men who compose that efficient arm of repression and order; they were stupid and sullen. And for that important moment they wore that peculiar expression of ludicrously fierce dignity that is affected by inferiors.

"What do you want?" I asked the sergeant.

He spoke excitedly in Spanish, which I didn't understand. Guessing that he had asked for my passport, I gave it to him.

Unfolding its maplike expanse, turning it this way and that and over and back, studying it at length and comprehending not a word, he folded it up in a complete mess and returned it.

"Your dispatch."

I gave him that. Whether he could read or not I do not know; it took him a long time. Finally, seemingly well satisfied, he gave it back to me. And then, fiercely and in Castillian that I clearly understood, he thundered—

"Take that flag down within five minutes."

Argument with one who couldn't understand was useless. I told him, smilingly, that the flag would not be lowered, pushed through the crowd and went aboard and below.

And that, until a few days later they flocked around like children, begging to be photographed, was the last we saw of the blood-curdling carabineros.

Little but the burying ground remains in commercial Port Harris to recall the glory of its Christian past. The wooden ecclesiastical buildings have been converted into offices, a store, a pool-room; the cabin cells have grown into dwelling houses, and these have multiplied and spread out over the half cleared environs in all the slovenly disorder of a busy frontier town. There is the squalor of where selfishness prevails instead of charity—and the exuberance of life.

A few miles eastward of the town is a lofty naked hive-shaped hill that flanks the

PORT HARRIS

entrance of the bay; and on its top, sharply silhouetted against the sky, stands a tiny Christian chapel. One day we started off afoot to visit it.

Our way led through stately groves of the southern evergreen and over rolling pastures following sheep paths that wandered aimlessly through a low growth of the thorny califata bush. The sheep were everywhere, and little lambs bleated and scampered before us. The hill rises abruptly many hundred feet from the surrounding plain; standing upon its top we overlooked the world.

It was a balmy golden day, and the long shadows of the afternoon lay across the land. The glistening town and its checkerboard of gardens and meadows, and the wharf and shipping, looked like a child's play village. To the north and west lay the flat pasture lands of Dawson Island; and from the warmth and seeming cultivation of this scene the eyes turned southward where, beyond a waste of bog and forest-covered foothills, stood the mountains wrapped in winter.

On the bare wind-swept summit of the hill was the chapel, a little wooden house silvered by rain and snow, dilapidated and abandoned, but with its rustic cross still at the gable end gleaming against the purple zenith. Within was nothing but the wooden walls and floor and roof, and the flimsy framework of a rail, and a rough altar built of hewn boards.

Yet on the walls of this dead church, that had been reared to wean the native from

(31)

his savage pleasure, the imperishable savagery of Christian men had scrawled as if in irony a kind of epitaph. Lovers had written up their names as a record of some happiness achieved behind the altar rail, and lonely souls had pictured their desires that others coming there might read them and be glad.

"Disgusting!" I said as the mate's sudden entrance startled me out of my vicarious pleasure: and, having perused the whole collection, I picked my way through the debris of broken communion-whiskey bottles that littered the floor and went out.

And all at once the golden beauty and the silence of that afternoon spoke nothing but the magnificence and utter heartlessness of God; and one was made to feel the pain of solitude. Man was not formed to bear it; and that his spirit yearns for contact with another is itself a mockery of solitude.

The sheep farms of Dawson Island were under the management of a Scotchman, Kenneth Morrison, who was established at the Estancia Valentine, twenty miles north of Port Harris. I have no sweeter memory than of our visit there.

Morrison had ridden to the port to meet us. He was a short powerful man of forty-five, rather taciturn, a pipe smoker given to long silences; yet by the subtle charm of his blunt manner and the veiled kindness of his blue eyes one was at once reminded of the affection with which everyone spoke of him. He was a solemn jester, and his invitation to us to "come and see the cannibals at Valentine" was characteristic of his way of concealing what came near his heart.

At noon of a clear grey day we set out together on horseback. For some miles the road led through the woods, giving the impression that we were penetrating the interior of the island, until, after a glimpse of the bay where we had lain one night at anchor, we emerged upon the coast, and its broad beach became our roadway. While our horses labored through the heavy sand, or picked a painful way over long gravel stretches, we were amused by Morrison's fantastic yarns, or, in the silences, thrilled by the wild bird life that abounded on the shore. Flocks of fat kelp-geese took to water as we neared them, and raced to sea with a frenzied flapping of their wings like motors. Small golden-brown hawks flew up in pairs and tamely perched on branches near enough to touch, and watched us pass.

Everywhere the shore was strewn with huge sawn logs awaiting transportation to the mill. We came upon a gang of men with bullocks hauling the logs down to the water's edge, and chaining them into a raft for the rising tide to float. A mile away we had heard this bullock gang at work, roaring and cursing. Armed with long poles, they seemed to struggle with the huge, slow-witted animals, beating and prodding them to pull together; and the wild energy and power of the living groups fitted the stark grandeur of the scene.

After some hours of riding along the beach we left it, and scrambling up the steep barranco to the higher land above, travelled again through woods and marshy stretches.

"Here," said Morrison solemnly as we ascended a hill, "is just halfway to my place."

And, as he continued with solicitous inquiries about our strength to go on, we reached the top, and saw below us, scarcely a mile away, amid smooth, cultivated fields, the brightly painted buildings of his farm.

Then down the hill and over the meadowlands we raced, and, with a pack of collies leaping and barking around us, reached the house. Our hostess came with a sweet grace to welcome us, and made our first arrival seem a homecoming.

The settlement of the farm stood, an oasis of cultivation, in the midst of a prairie bordering on the sea. Surrounded by flower gardens with neat borders and gravel paths, the house was as the countenance of quiet happiness. And the security and warmth, the studied comforts and the homely luxuries within fulfilled that thought and told what peace could be achieved in the most utter solitude.

Not the least source of amusement to the Morrisons were his eternal jokes; and that they had never destroyed her simple belief in him was evidence of his own predominating kindness. At dinner Morrison produced a little phial of oil of cloves.

"What is that, Kenneth?" said his wife, noticing it.

"That," he replied, "is something that makes you young."

And we entered together upon a discussion of the miraculous properties of what we alleged to be a highly concentrated glandular fluid obtained from crude petroleum, a true elixir of life.

"The contents of that bottle, Mrs. Morrison," I said, "if taken in one dose, would make a man of, say, forty-five a youth of sixteen."

Mrs. Morrison looked for a moment incredulously at our stolid faces.

"Kenneth!" she cried in a sudden panic of belief, seizing his arm that held the phial. "Don't take too much of it!"

That night before the open grate with those kind people there beside us, conversing of their interests, of their tranquil daily life complete with ordered occupation, I thought that here indeed, in this remote and solitary place, was happiness.

And yet for what comfort was she reading books on "New Thought," and what did Morrison conceal behind his jesting? Even the very bliss of peace evokes the sorrow of reflection.

It was late afternoon of a most lovely day that, heavy-hearted as at leaving home, we rode away. Morrison again came with us, for we had grown close. The strait was quiet as a mountain lake, and in the south, beyond its turquoise plain, the snowy ranges glowed flamingo-red against a lemon sky. While the high peaks still flamed, the full golden moon came up beside them, so that no darkness followed, and the night became a quieter reflection of the day. There never was a night more beautiful.

Morrison stayed with us until the day before we sailed. Then he jumped on his horse, cried, "Don't let the cannibals eat you!" laughed, and galloped off. I walked quickly away. Suddenly I stopped and looked back. Morrison, far off, that very instant reined his horse and turned. Each with one impulse raised an arm. Farewell!

Meanwhile, under skilled hands, the repairs to the *Kathleen* were progressing. A further injury that she had sustained while being drawn up on to the slip had revealed her fundamental weakness. The cradle that had been built for that operation had not been properly designed and the boat's whole weight came to rest upon two points. Her thin sides and ribs yielding to that concentrated pressure were bent in abruptly as much as four inches. By mere good fortune she was not stove. Nevertheless, it was a disclosure of the fact that her hull was entirely too light in construction to withstand such strains as her weight and the pressure of her sails would subject her to. Examination showed this weakness to have been responsible for our mishap on the day of sailing, for several streaks of planking on both sides had been sprung apart. She was like a sieve. I think that in the whole course of our adventures we had no moment of discouragement so black as when we beheld the forlorn *Kathleen* emerging from the water, with her sides bent in and water streaming out from every seam. And others showed discouragement since, for the last damage, the shipyard men were entirely at fault.

That night the iconoclastic manager of the Port Harris establishment, Señor Marcou, called upon us. It was pouring rain, and we were seated in the little cabin which, owing to the cradle having been removed from under the boat, was tilted at an uncomfortable angle of about thirty degrees. Señor Marcou was a rotund, red-cheeked, bright-eyed, jovial Frenchman, demonstrative, kind, irascible, and—as he proved to us—a generous and entertaining host. "Look out for Marcou," they'd said in Punta Arenas—but they'd say anything. Little of his vivacity was revealed that dreary night that he first called to pay his respects: the burden of some responsibility for our boat's condition weighed heavily on his mind.

"What can we do about your boat?" he asked at once.

We asked for very little—and he gave us everything.

"Well," he said finally, "we'll give your boat a thorough overhauling and make it fit to go to the Horn in."

"But I can't pay for it!" I exclaimed.

"No matter," he replied laughingly, "and now come home to dinner."

And so it happened that for two weeks we were the guests of that good fellow, lunching and dining daily at his house, and, regularly twice a week, visiting the movies, where we sat aloft in the frigid managerial box and looked at faded, flickering pictures of puff-sleeved romances of pre-Spanish-war days.

There was little that I could do to repay such hospitality; but one service presented itself. The greatest achievement of Dawson's shipworks was the construction of Chile's *Great Eastern*, the auxiliary conglomerate, *Sara*. Her glorious launching had marked the realization of her constructors' highest dreams of achievement, and her

(34)

THE *KATHLEEN* OF NEW YORK

untimely death by fire was their grave. Dawson lived upon the memory of *Sara*. And that time might never dim for them the recollection of her glory I would paint her portrait.

An unused photographic studio was put at my disposal and I went to work. Construction plans, photographs, the counsel of everyone that had worked on the ship or seen her, were at my disposal. Upon a dark green sea, against a background of the gleaming snow peaks of Dawson and a thunder dark sky, I put her, sailing, all sails set, before the wind; and in the foreground, heedless of anachronism, appeared the little *Kathleen*. As the main body of the ship was brought to correctness, I began upon such an elaboration of details as only the infallible records of the plans and the loving, all-cherishing memories of the ship's creators could have suggested: to the last block and halyard, and the smallest detail of the electric winch, to the captain's uniform and the contour of the cook's nose, all, all, as I was told of them, I painted on.

"Lindo, lindo!" cried Marcou, as quarter-hourly he ran to watch my progress.

The fame of my portrait of the incomparable *Sara* soon spread to every house, and my work became constantly interrupted by crowds of curious, enthusiastic sightseers. But, being through my ignorance of Spanish unable to understand a word that was said, I became after a time almost oblivious to their presence and could finally hold doggedly to my work in the very midst of a riotous and pushing mob.

There was only one group of visitors that became intolerable, my friends the carabineros. Every day they called, clamoring for prints of the pictures I had taken of them. And their demands were beyond all reason; indeed, considering my limited stock of materials, impossible. In vain did I try with gestures to explain my feelings in the matter. They only talked the more volubly, stupidly oblivious to my not understanding anything. It is singularly disturbing, even humiliating, to be addressed persistently in a strange tongue. You feel bereft of dignity and utterly and unworthily stupid.

After careful consideration of this problem I hit upon the expedient of swiftly reversing the situation by pouring out a torrent of English upon my annoyers, and observed the effect with much amusement. But still they came, these carabineros.

Finally, one day about the hour they were due, I locked the door. They came, they knocked, they thundered. There was a peeking through cracks, and a low-toned consultation; then redoubled thundering. The view of the interior of the place was obscured by opaque glass that went to half the windows' height; but above this and along the whole long side of the room were the clear lights. Presently I heard a bumping and a rumbling. Casks were being brought! They stood these in a row and mounted them; and I beheld those five, dull, ugly faces peering in on me. Never before had I guessed my power of concentration. By not the flicker of an eye did I betray my knowledge of their presence there—but calmly proceeded with my painting of the forty-eight little stars of the American flag at the *Kathleen's* peak—wishing that soldier's wits might comprehend the irony of that.

(36)

While down at the harbor they were bracing, riveting, bolting, caulking, painting the *Kathleen*, there was I rebuilding, as it were, the *Sara*. And when at last I bore her triumphantly, with all flags flying, to Marcou, then, on that very day, the *Kathleen* slid down from the ways and floated in her element again.

CHAPTER VI

SLAUGHTER COVE

SAILING had become to us an event of such rare occurrence, and had thus far been the prelude of such dramatic and almost catastrophic happenings that, if the interest of our friends with its expression of farewells and cheers had not given it the color of a festival, the excitement of our own tumultuous fears and hopes would alone have made for us the weighing of our anchor one of life's high moments.

Three weeks had passed like one; and although the hospitality of Dawson had showed no signs of waning and its simple ways and wonders, rather than wearying us might have become our habit for as many months, our boat was finished. She was, as it was said, fit for the Horn; and, as if the Horn were that consummation to which our lives were purposed, it held us by a law stronger than the allurements of pleasant ease.

What forces drive men on to the deliberate quest of miseries and danger? Are they remote yet deeply rooted habits of a race which once delighted in adventure for the gain it held, that still assert themselves against the very soul's desire for peace and the mind's clear understanding of the paths that lead there? Is it a far-visioned life-force maintaining itself against the disintegrating allurements of ease, a militant expression of the subconscious will that's cognizant of individual weakness, an assertion in contraries of the complex of inferiority? Is bravery the cloak of cowardice?

Loving the crowd too much and shunning solitude we seek it. Fearing our own selves' insufficiency we must forever make a trial of it alone. Because of all things we desire slothfully to lie abed we are possessed with energy to be about before the dawn. Never, it seems to have been willed, may men enjoy that happiness their souls desire.

(38)

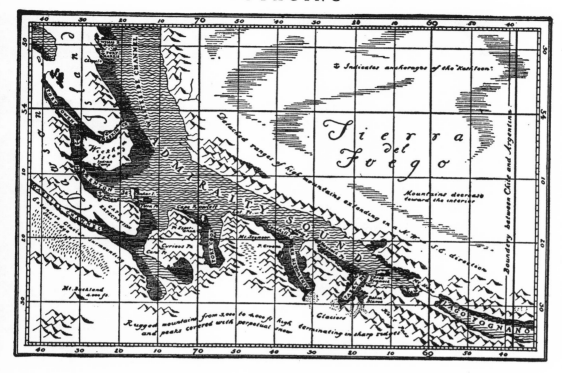

So, in the enthusiasm of the great humbug of rejoicing, amid the farewells of friendships that are real, toasted and blessed and laden with gifts, we sail away. The schooners in the harbor dip their flags, the sawmill whistle shrieks. We're off! Port Harris is a bank of waving hands—then a memory.

There was a strong east wind abeam and a choppy sea, and the sky was heavy and threatening. Tree Bluff, bare, brown and huge, stood over us as we left the bay, a mountain dome above a wilderness of forest. Southward of that the coast was ever wilder and more mountainous. White summits touched the leaden sky and under them the somber green and purple forests clothed the slopes.

After five hours of tumultuous sailing we entered the sheltered waters of Meskim Channel, the mountain shores drew close and towered over us, and suddenly it was vastly quiet as if all sound and movement in the world had stopped, and we heard only the silver rippling of the wavelets on our sides as the soft wind bore us on. Then living creatures came to welcome us. There was a quick soft momentary tearing of the water, and another and again; and porpoises were all about us, playing like young dogs. They leaped and darted back and forth across our bows, or followed at our side, or dove beneath the keel, rolling white bellies that glowed like emeralds through the clear depths.

(39)

Thus gloriously escorted, we proceeded, sailing quietly, to where, at a narrowing of the channel as it turned, we found a most peaceful little crescent cove, clean beached and forest bordered, utterly remote and still; on the wind's last breath we entered there and anchored.

For days we loitered at that anchorage unwilling to forsake a spot that one might choose to spend a lifetime in. Then, too, it was dead calm. At nightfall it began to rain. All night it poured and all the morning of the following day, a cold dreary rain that fell from winter altitudes and chilled us, so that we loved best the snug dry world of the boat's cabin.

And then it cleared. And the warm sun came out so beautifully that the wind held its breath as if in awe of the world's loveliness. We embarked in the little skiff and rowed for miles through water so tranquil that the mountains were reflected in it to the minutest detail of their splendour; and by the low sun was revealed such a wonderland of rocks and streams and groves above the distant shore, as set us flaming with desire to claim it for ourselves and make it habitable. We thought of home-steads there on some entrancing cove, with rustic bridges to the little islands, and landing places, and cultivated fields and meadowlands and gardens—it is so easy for the mind to make an Eden of the distant wilderness.

Such was that distant shore; yet at our backs, crowding the narrow beach on which we stood, we might observe its counterpart without illusion. It was a dense and tangled forest, with the sodden bog that was its soil cluttered with fallen trunks and rankly overgrown with thorny underbrush. It was a jungle that only some dire necessity of man would ever venture to reclaim. All things look good from far away; and it is man's eternally persistent childlike faith in the reality of that illusion that has made him the triumphant restless being that he is.

Always the farthest peaks appear the fairest, and if again we weighed our anchor and to the gentle east wind spread our sail, it was only that the very glories of what we had seen stimulated our faith in unimaginable beauties that must lie beyond.

It was the faintest breeze that bore us up the channel the morning that we sailed; the sun shone for a little while; and then, into the clear blue field of heaven there stole so many little fleecelike clouds, like sheep cropping their way over virgin pasture, that at last their flocks covered the firmament as with a woolen mantle and hid the sun. And with the greyness there fell a breathless hush over the world.

We had reached the western point of Wickam Island where Meskim Channel joins Brenton Sound to form there the broad fiord known as Port Owen that penetrates the heart of Dawson Island almost to the western shore. Its whole unbroken expanse was before us to the far-off, snow-topped mountain range that closed its end. In that fiord alone were wonders of wild mountain scenery to have held one there for weeks of exploration. But the wind had failed us and we yielded to the current of a strong ebb tide and let our boat be borne through the archipelago of little islands that cluster

around the extremity of Wickam Island. Southward we proceeded through a maze of these, without a wind, seemingly so motionless on the calm breast of the tide that it appeared as if the land streamed past us to display itself.

It was late afternoon when, having emerged from the hundred islands into the broad water of Brenton Sound, we came abreast of a promising anchorage behind a reef. We pulled the *Kathleen* to a berth behind the shelter of a screen of trees, dropped anchor and moored her to the shore; and again, at rest in this remote and quiet solitude, by virtue of the comforts of our boat at home in it, we felt profound security and peace.

And it appeared to be not alone the human spirit that felt the security of that hour and place. Wild fowl, quite unaccustomed to the intrusions of man, swam fearlessly about, and a most loving pair of ducks circled tranquilly around the boat delighting in their mated happiness. For a long time we observed them with great pleasure, and then, from some strange ugly depths in us or a perverted fancy of the mind, the will arose to kill them. Waiting for a moment that brought them close together, the mate at one shot killed them both. We plucked them of their glossy plumage and threw the feathers overboard. The tide was slack, and, as if to force upon us a recognition of the sacrilege we had committed, the feathers and the blood-clouded water clung about us until almost dark. Undoubtedly, there is in man the lust to kill; but there is, too, a loathing for it that flows from the source of all human kindness and response to beauty.

At twilight there came a sudden and unnatural darkness. Black clouds hung low over the mountains and from them burst a hurricane and wind that in ten minutes churned the placid surface of the sound into a seething maelstrom of white water. The spray flew over us like driving rain; and from the close shelter of the cabin we listened to the whistling and the whipping of the shrouds and halyards and the spiteful lapping of the wind-swept tide against our sides.

So, furiously, for an hour the gale raged, and then was quiet. And at bedtime through the broken clouds the stars appeared, showing with dazzling brightness through the wind clean spaces. Night cleaned the heavens and left them cloudless for the dawning of another day.

At sunrise, while breakfast was in preparation, we took advantage of the faint breeze that stirred, weighed anchor and sailed out. Leaving that anchorage with memories of the night before, we named it Slaughter Cove.

CHAPTER VII

"CANNIBALS"

OF the many hundred Indians who, as has been told, once populated Dawson Island, there remain five; and these, being of that particularly savage Alacaloof race that still sparsely inhabits the channel islands, or, more exactly, the *channels* off the extreme southern mainland of Chile—persisting there in the utter degradation of their pristine savagery and the enjoyment of their unregenerate and naked misery—these five came then to the channels of Dawson Island of their own volition, as to a hunting ground that might sustain them. And it does; they live. Where, in which one of the remote fiords and inlets of the extensive region of Dawson Island and the adjacent mainland, this wild band might be encountered no one could tell us; for a long time they had not been seen. Yet our adventurous imaginations had been so stimulated by everything we had read or been told of the treachery and murderous depravity of the channel Indians that we hurried with reckless curiosity to meet with them. And it was with this ardent hope that we had deviated from the straight course of our voyage to explore the waters about Wickam Island.

It was a cloudless morning that we sailed again and the sun shone with the grateful warmth of a fair day in early spring, for October is our April in the Southern Hemisphere. Above the mountains of the south of Dawson that rose from the far shore of Brenton Sound appeared a distant table-land of ice and snow so lofty and so vast in its extent, and so unmarked with any break or peak to give it scale, that it dwarfed those nearer heights, which, seen on the clouded yesterday standing alone against the sky, had seemed immense. It was the ice-capped region south of Gabriel Channel that we saw.

WICKAM ISLAND

We had heard a vague report of an almost unknown canal that extended clear through Dawson Island from Brenton Sound to Gabriel Channel, making two islands of what appeared on the charts as one. That we should find errors in the charts was not improbable. Large tracts of this far southwestern land-and-water region have been only superficially surveyed, and future exploration will undoubtedly reveal more intricacies of that tortuous geography.

We crossed the blue sound to a deep bay that appeared on its southern shore and which, by the disposition of the mountains around it, suggested the existence there of that mysterious passage which we hoped to find. The faint wind failed us entirely as we made the entrance, and we came to anchor. Although quite obviously land enclosed, the mate, not satisfied, embarked in the skiff and rowed off toward the head of the bay that lay southeasterly two miles away where a valley opened inland. And through the hours that he was gone I sprawled about on deck in the sensual enjoyment, there in early spring in that far-famed worst region in the world, of such delicious warmth of sunshine, and such Alpine and Pacific splendours of white mountain tops, and green forests and blue sea, as the imagination of man ever awakened to desire.

On the mate's return, he reported that the bay terminated in shoals and flats and

(44)

that a stream entered there up which he had been able to take the skiff some little way; and that on the shore where the stream joined the bay were the frames of the Indian wigwams. And at that our hopes beat high.

We sailed again and beat a few miles to the eastward, anchoring after nightfall in an almost landlocked cove.

Next day in the semi-darkness of a clouded dawn we made the open water, and with the wind continuing faint and contrary worked our way slowly down the sound.

It was near noon. The day had settled into dreary greyness. From time to time it rained and simultaneously grew dead calm as if the feeble wind lacked strength to penetrate the curtain of the falling drops; and the monotonous whispering of the rain, absorbing the whole universe of lesser sounds, became itself as the immense silence of a lifeless world.

Suddenly, from the far-off forest of the dark mountain side across the water, faintly through the falling shroud of rain, alone and clear above the silence, came the barking of a dog.

The solitude was gone: The dog's voice spoke the presence in that wilderness of man; and in an instant our imaginations peopled the dark shadows of the forest with lurking savages; felt eyes peering at us stealthily through the interstices. And the succeeding silence became the ominous hush of treachery.

The rain ceased. The wind came; darkening the water. From the edge of the forest of the northern shore arose a column of smoke. We steered for it.

Staring through the glasses we discovered two overturned boats on the beach, and above them in the shadows of the trees two huts. Presently, as we drew nearer, there appeared against the darkness of the doorways two faces peering out, each luminous and round and motionless as a moon. A man came out and strolled down to the boats.

One long tack carried us a few yards to leeward of the settlement. We dropped anchor there; and while we put our deck to rights the man on the shore, who had been watching us attentively, walked up abreast of us and stood at the water's edge continuing his scrutiny. To our hail he made no reply.

While we were tremendously excited at thus fortunately encountering cannibals, there was nothing in the appearance of things to warrant any course but that which instinctive courtesy prescribed for a chance meeting between human beings in the wilderness. So, putting into my pocket a few cakes of the greatest delicacy that our stores contained, Huyler's chocolate emergency ration, I embarked with the mate for the shore.

The silent being there awaited us, and, as we landed, gave us a helping hand to draw the skiff above the water's reach.

He was a man of about sixty, as well as one can judge the age of strangers of an unfamiliar race. He was of medium height and powerful big-bellied build, and was

INDIAN COVE

clad in filthy tattered and patched remnants of a miscellaneous assortment of white men's garments. His skin was swarthy. The face was broad, flat-nosed, with small eyes wide apart. He had good teeth, small, widely spaced and jagged. Altogether, his countenance if not beaming with good will was quite free of sinister expression. He was unassumingly at ease with us, not over curious, and entirely friendly. We shook his hard-skinned pudgy hand and greeted him.

"Very bad weather," he remarked in a horrible dialect which he later referred to as Castilian.

And from this strikingly familiar opening of conversation he proceeded, as we sauntered down the beach, to ask for gifts—tobacco, flour, sugar.

As we approached the dwellings another man, a younger one, came out and leaned against the boats. He nodded to us. He was lame, and his right arm was crippled. He showed it to me. It was so terribly inflamed and swollen from the fingers to the elbow that I could make nothing of the cause.

Meanwhile, as we stood conversing on the shingle below the huts, the two moon faces, unperturbed, looked at us from the darkness of their doorways. They were of

(46)

two women, somberly clad, each seated on her threshold with her knees drawn up in that posture of patient endurance and unconscious contemplation of the ancient seers of William Blake. The huts, or wigwams as they should perhaps be called, stood side by side in the grass that bordered the shingle. Over them hung the low limbs of the forest trees, giving them shelter from the wind and rain at the expense of such warmth as the occasional sun might offer. They were as similar as two bird's nests and not unlike them in the primitive yet entirely substantial method of their construction. About a ten-foot circle small sapling poles had been stuck into the ground. These were then bent archlike toward the center and secured with bindings of grass. Other poles were warped diagonally about this skeleton dome and bound at the intersection to give the structure strength. It was covered with skins and rags of canvas and close-leafed boughs of the *coigue* tree, leaving an aperture for entrance on the side that faced the sea and one at the apex for the escape of smoke. The sides were banked with sod and grass to a foot's height.

One of the guardians of the doorway appeared to be very old; her face was wrinkled and her hair thin and white. She spoke no "Castilian," but conversed, from time to time, in rich guttural tones in the native tongue. The other woman was about forty. Her voice, too, was deep and rich, with a mournful monotony of cadence; and the expression of her face was at once impressively sad and kind. This younger woman stood to let us enter. She was tall and lithe and had a manner of great dignity.

True dignity is a grace of the spirit that transcends all limitations of age and race and birth and opportunity; it is bestowed, as it were, out of the universal loving-kindness of God as a visible token of that noble order of beings who, respecting themselves and reverencing the unknown, have achieved maturity within themselves.

A fire of logs burned in the center of the wigwam. On either side were beds of skins matted into cozy human-nestlike hollows by long days and nights of sleeping in them. On the ground behind the fire lay a hunk of half-dried sea-lion meat, the leg of a guanaco and the carcass of an enormous Fuegian rat, the *coati*. A well-made grass basket and a Winchester rifle were the only utensils or implements there. It was warm and dry within that wigwam; and there is no doubt that even in the most severe winter weather one could be more comfortable in such a native shelter and live with more economy of fuel and labor than in any temporary house a white man might construct.

The boats that lay on the shore were dilapidated and, one would say, unseaworthy. One was a cast-off flat-bottomed white man's skiff, the other a rough thing of similar model built of wide boards of driftwood. And yet the coati and the remains of gua-naco that we had seen showed that these people had recently crossed, if not the wide and treacherous sound from Tierra del Fuego, at least the considerable bodies of water that indent the south shore of Admiralty Sound.

I had distributed my gifts of chocolate. The Indians were neither impressed by my

(47)

generosity nor curious about what the silver-covered packages contained. They thanked me and either pocketed them or laid them aside. The younger woman asked me for soap.

We returned to the *Kathleen* accompanied by the old man. While we assembled an assortment of supplies for him, he waited, seated on the deck, looking abjectly forlorn and filthy amid the trim surroundings of the boat. We bestowed upon him a fair quantity of tobacco, flour, sugar, soap powder, beans, matches and bread. He thanked us with quiet politeness, saying, "Not much, but very good."

It seemed to me when finally I had brought this savage back to the shore and stood there with him for a moment at our parting, that there was little evidence of an abyss of centuries between us. Miserably poor in goods, slothful, and filthy with neglect, he was the type of his race; yet among the enlightened races of the earth are individuals, and even classes, whom circumstances or temperament have reduced to apparently that same condition, or who, in reaction to the pace of civilization, to its burdens and responsibilities, yearn for the freedom of vagabondage. How thin a veneer upon the deep substratum of humanity must our culture be when, through desire or circumstances, men can so easily revert ten thousand years!

We waved farewell as we sailed off, but there was no response. From those dark doorways in the shadow of the forest the two moons again looked out, as if eternally. And if they saw us it could only be that by the course we took we crossed their fixed and far-off seaward vision. So little did we count: had we been gods we only should have known it.

That afternoon a little before dark, we entered Indian Cove on the south shore of Brenton Sound, and anchored there; and for two nights and a whole day we continued at that anchorage. It was dead calm and the rain fell as gently as a mist, and murmured on the glassy surface of the water. From the forest came the sweet trilling of little birds. Flocks of wild ducks and geese fed on the flats or swam about us. Kingfishers flashed their courtship: it was the mating season, and of the very stillness was the breath of love.

A little river empties into that cove. Above its broad and shallow mouth it flows from mountain heights by falls and rapids through a deep ravine in the darkness of the overarching forest. With great difficulty I made my way on foot along the bank. Luxuriant parasitic growth encumbers the forest; mosses and small plants grow thick upon the lower trunks of living trees, whose roots, as if in struggle to escape from strangulation, rear themselves out of the mucky soil, until unbalanced by their own rank growth of foliage and the encumbering weight of clinging vines and fungi, they fall—and are engulfed in the devouring vegetation.

The forest floor is many tiered, a structure built of trunks fallen crosswise upon fallen trunks, a sodden, rotting mass of barriers all overgrown with greenery, with pits between choked up with thorny underbrush.

SAILING FREE

Making so little progress here, I struggled up the steep sides of the ravine to a hilltop free of trees that held our hope of better footing. Yet even there, under last season's matted growth of grass, was bog as saturated as the spongy hollows of the forest.

On the shores of Indian Cove were the remains of several encampments identical with that living one that we had visited. With the long grass grown up about their trampled hollows they resembled the twin nests of some huge bird. The framework of one pair was still intact. They stood in a most green and pleasant grove beside a little rill of water, and like those others, faced the water.

One could fancy dwelling there in the achievement of that leisure which is the heart's desire; and, from the hut's snug warmth and darkness, contemplating hours long, for days and years, that most absolute, unchanging and eternal universe of sea and mountain peaks and stars, until at last thought ripened into understanding.

"I then asked Ezekiel," writes Blake of a conversation with the prophet, "why he ate dung, and lay so long on his right and left side. He answer'd, 'The desire of raising other men into a perception of the infinite': this the North American tribes practise, and is he honest who resists his genius or conscience only for the sake of present ease or gratification?"

(49)

We, to whom the struggle for material comforts has become an obsession, have vauntingly named our pathway progress: our struggle may, however, be as well considered to have been a degenerate weakening, under the pressure of material discomforts, of the will toward leisure—a weakening that became a rout, a rout that we to save our pride name purpose—a purpose whose achievement in the denial of leisure we call civilization. And now at last, having become utterly and irretrievably involved in the disaster of materialism and having debauched the human soul with restlessness, we make luxury our glory, and abandon leisure to the childhood of the race.

The second night in Indian Cove it cleared. Fierce wind squalls beat down from the mountain tops, careening us and howling in our rigging. The water rippled angrily against the boat's sides. The wind had changed.

CHAPTER VIII

"ROLL ON"

WE turned out early, in that portentous hour that precedes the dawn. Above mountainous dark land the cloudless sky was luminous with stars; it was a breathless morning, clear and sweet. Then imperceptibly the daylight came and the gold of sunrise flung itself across the heavens, kindled the mountain peaks and overflowed the world. A gentle wind arose and bore us out. O fresh, clear, fair west wind! That day we blessed it, and the next —and then for five interminable wind-bound weeks we cursed its obstinacy.

With the fair wind and freshening, and bright wind clouds streaming up across the sky, we sailed down Brenton Sound and passed the channel south of the Tucker Islands. Before us, due east by the compass, lay the green-blue length of Admiralty Sound, white-capped and swept by purple shadows. The sun shone dazzling bright on snowy peaks and glistening walls of rock, displaying all the details of the land in crystal clarity—bare golden hills, and shaded wonderlands of forest, and dark ravines that gushed out silver streams. It was a day so opulently beautiful that the pure exuberance of the wind and the sun induced intoxication.

Eastward of Cape Rowlett the land becomes increasingly abrupt and mountainous. Dwarfed, wind-worn forests, sparsely clothe the slopes. The naked structure of the land appears, rock faces broken sheer or glacier worn, vast slopes of ledge and gravel, stunted underbrush upon the middle heights, and plains of bog; and, on the summits, snow. Through gaps in that shore's mountain wall appear the lofty peaks and the snow-clad southern ranges, whose ice-choked valleys spill out glaciers down the hollows of the slopes.

At the head of Ainsworth Harbor there was visible to us, as we passed the entrance,

CORKHILL ISLAND

a glacier huge as a frozen Mississippi. The eddies and churned currents of that ice stream score its broad surface with the forms of a flowing torrent. It breaks off at the water's edge in cliffs of translucent turquoise.

All day we sailed with a great wind astern that sometimes mounted to a gale. Those seas to our small boat were mountains high. They followed us as if to overwhelm us; they overtook and lifted us, and left us, foaming as they went.

There are few harbors along that precipitous shore, and in the miles between them scarcely a beach or sheltered point where one could land. Accordingly, when, with the afternoon not far advanced and the wind still holding strong, we elected to pass by Ainsworth Harbor and continue up the sound, we put before us a good two hours' sailing to reach the next anchorage, Parry Harbor. And that with a wind so fair and steady we should reach there in broad daylight we had no doubt. But wise men do not rely on the wind.

Within two hours it was calm, dead glassy calm; and in the long smooth swell of the subsiding sea we rocked and drifted helplessly about not two miles from the headland at the harbor's mouth. So on our helplessness the day went out; the shadow of the far-off western mountain sides extinguishing at last the highest flaming peaks. And night descended chill and bleak, and then the wind.

(52)

HAYCOCK POINT

As we turned the headland the wind beat down in violent and variable squalls. It was impossible to see. We drove on into that darkness, trusting to what the chart obscurely showed of the coast's contour. For a few minutes we steered due south; then, estimating that we had come abreast of Stanley Cove, we proceeded to beat in short tacks straight at the abysmal midnight of the mountain side. Someone in speaking of this anchorage had told us of two rocks that we must pass between. With straining eyes we saw them straight before us. Sailing close hauled it seemed that by a narrow margin we could make the passage. Suddenly, with a howl of fury, the squall veered. We hung in stays a moment drifting onto the leeward rock. With swift presence of mind, the mate threw the tiller hard to windward. We slacked the sheet and bore away to clear the danger; we escaped that shipwreck by a fathom's clearance.

Somehow, aided by incessant sounding, we navigated safely that dark entrance to the cove, and, finding bottom at last, anchored in five fathoms of water.

While the mate set things on board to rights, I launched the skiff, and rowed out into that midnight to discover and explore the shore. I skirted the rocks for perhaps a quarter of a mile before encountering a landing place. There on a pebble beach, I drew the skiff ashore, and stood at last, after a voyage of near seven thousand miles,

(53)

STANLEY COVE

on grim Tierra del Fuego. I felt the stony shore under my feet, and the deep bog moss and the ferns that bordered it. Darkly appeared against the starlit sky the tossing silhouette of wind-torn trees; a mountain towered over me, immense and black. Snow was on the slopes not far away. It was cold, and the wind roared through the forest tops.

My soul was stirred by the vast glamour of that unseen wilderness, with fear of the terrific forces of the darkness, with wonder at what world the night concealed, with pride at the achievement of my being there, and with utter humility at my alien identity, diminutive, obscure, unseen in that boundless solitude beneath the stars.

With a strong fair wind we sailed next morning for the head of Admiralty Sound. The day was overcast and sullen; a dark sea lashed itself to gleaming foam against the frowning headlands of the coast. Sheer mountain sides here form the northern slope; they rise in cliffs a thousand feet in height, between whose pinnacled and spired summits pour streams and glaciers from a loftier snow-clad hinterland. It is a heartless, bleak coast; it was a tragic coast under that day's dark threat of storm.

The land at the head of Admiralty Sound is split by two valleys bearing easterly, a divided continuance of that chasm of the earth which is the sound. Between them, extending into the sound, to form two bays, stands Mount Hope, the western end of

(54)

a ten-mile rocky range that terminates where the two valleys dip and join again to make the bed of the great inland lake, Fognano. Mount Hope appears from the sound to stand alone, a dome of rock detached from all the mountains of the region.

The southern bay lies open to the full fury of the west wind and the sea. A little treeless island two miles from the head, and near the shore, affords the only anchorage.

Although the wind was strong, to save manœuvring we jibbed to come about behind the island. And here, through my land-lubberly awkwardness in the handling of the congested intricacies of tiller and sheet at the cramped stern of our double-ender, the adventures of me nearly came to an untimely and inglorious end. The hurtling main-boom struck me with terrific force, hurling me backwards over the combing. I clutched and held to God knows what and hung, half in the water, a little more ashamed than scared, and far more scared than hurt.

However, we had come about, and continuing a little further on that tack we shot up into the wind and anchored in the calmer water of the island's lee.

On the shore of the bay, half a mile from where we lay, stood the buildings and enclosures of a sheep farm. Rowing ashore we proceeded there on foot. It was a small establishment, a house, a ramshackle shed or two, and the fenced corral and labyrinth of the dip. The surrounding plain was hidden with the charred stumps of a forest that had once stood there; and it was evidence of the short-sightedness of the human occupants of the place that the destruction of the trees had left the buildings exposed to the unbroken violence of the western gales. Over the sheep-cropped grass about the house was strewn a litter of filth and bones and rotting carcasses. Two condors left their carrion gorge as we approached and on huge wings raised themselves to mountain heights and soared away.

With the cold wind whistling about us, filling our eyes with drifting sand, we circled round the house in vain for signs of life within. Then, balked of that hospitality and the warm cup of coffee we had promised ourselves, we set off briskly for the head of the bay.

That southern valley in which we now were terminates at the sound in a broad, flat, sandy plain, that the pasturing of sheep has converted from a moss-grown waste into a close-cropped lawn of grass. A sand dune separates it from the shore and shelters it a little from prevailing winds. Between its nothern border and the range of Mount Hope flows a deep, swift stream, broadening near its outlet so as to afford a roomy anchorage for a boat of the tonnage of ours; and it was with a view to shifting the *Kathleen* to that berth that we went to reconnoiter it.

It was high tide when we reached the river bank, and the sea having entered the lower reaches of the stream had deepened and broadened it and assimilated its current, so that we beheld a most inviting, almost landlocked, little harbor.

"Absolutely perfect!" we cried; and we hurried down to inspect the entrance.

This was not so good. It narrowed abruptly when it entered the sea to a passage

A CLOSER LOOK AT HAYCOCK POINT

not more than thirty feet in width, with a cliff on one side of it and a steep sand bank on the other. Outside, on one hand were reefs and on the other the long curved beach of the bay with the sea thundering along it. To all appearances, at that hour of high tide, with the surface of the water torn by the wind, there was depth enough outside for a straight approach. It was worth chancing in preference to continuing at the wind-raked anchorage where we lay.

On our return we found the tenant of the farm at home. And now, lest these pages come to glow with that too kindly spirit of undiscriminating love for man, I permit myself the happiness of presenting this mealy-mouthed hypocrite as the pernicious scoundrel that he was.

There are all kinds of scoundrels. We have the individualists who, sinning against the law, get rich, or go to jail, or hang—and there's an end of them; there are the democratic scoundrels who, holding that one man is as good as another, sin against God, whose worship is "honoring his gifts, in other men, each according to his genius, and loving the greatest men best: those who envy or calumniate great men hate God." Irreverence is the *greatest* sin. But there remains that most inhuman sin of all, inhospitality.

If Gómez had been a weak, dyspeptic, suffering creature, whose own misery had poisoned the wells of kindness within him, there would have been cause enough, out of the hatefulness of life as he experienced it, to justify unbridled spleen against the world; but he was neither weak nor ill. He was a powerful and stocky fellow, brown skinned and bearded like a ruffian of romance. He hadn't mean and shifty eyes, but rather placid ox-like orbs that looked at me unfalteringly. Gómez was at peace with God and with himself, we came to know; and he observed his Christian fellowship with all the prayerful jumping, shouting, clapping, moaning, rolling, bouncing, sobbing imbecility of a Holy-jumper.

"Enter," said Gómez with a grimace of hospitality, when I had presented to him a warm letter of introduction from his employer, Señor Marcou, in which every attention and courtesy was bespoken. "We would ask you to partake of a meal with us, but we have so little to offer," and, ingratiatingly rubbing his hands, he proceeded to tell us that he abstained from wine and tobacco, and from the flesh of the "sinful" guanaco, and that he received four hundred pesos a month wages and free food and clothing. And all the while he talked we heard through the thin partition of the next room the incessant droning moaning of one praying aloud. Presently it ceased. There was the sound of a body bestirring itself and, with the great bulk filling the doorway, the prayerful one appeared.

"My dear wife," said Gómez, introducing her.

This saintly woman's face resembled a gorilla's; the eyes were small and close set, the nose was flat, and the whole skull projected toward an immense and shapeless orifice of mouth that opened and shut like a trap.

The house was untidy and unclean and almost empty. On the kitchen wall hung two framed Bible texts, and in the prayer-chamber bedroom was the broad, long, deep, soft couch of a voluptuary, laid with sheepskins, blankets, counterpanes, and the downy robes of sinful, wild guanacos.

"Very bad weather," said Gómez. "Very bad country; very bad pasture; very bad year for sheep; very bad men around here. Mulach at Lago Fognano very bad man, always drunk." (Muy mal hombre; siempre borracho!)

We questioned him about the anchorage in the river, telling him that we intended moving our boat to it. He laughed and, with obscure significance, shrugged his shoulders, avoiding a direct reply.

"Tomorrow," he said in obedience to a command in the letter I had presented, "I take you to the lake."

Both because of the tide's effect upon the river current and that it might favor us in the event of our running aground, we hoped to postpone the attempt to enter the river until the flood tide had set in. The day was, however, so overcast that at five o'clock, with darkness threatening, we hove anchor. The strong wind bore us with what seemed incredible speed toward the land, whose long, low shore appeared of unbroken extent, revealing nothing of the river's mouth save the cliff that marked it.

(57)

MACY ISLAND

It had been high tide when we inspected the seaward approach, and the water had appeared to be of even and sufficient depth. Now, however, as we drew nearer to the land we observed breakers as far from shore as half a mile. Nevertheless, from what had been told us of the river, and particularly from Gómez' having mentioned no dangers, it seemed reasonable to continue; so, with white seas everywhere to starboard of us and reefs and a converging rocky shore to port, we held on straight for the narrow river mouth. Suddenly the water under us showed a pallid green. The mate leaped forward to observe the depth: it was too late. A long sea broke across our bows. There was no room to turn, nor time; we struck.

A foaming sea swept by us, grinding us along. Another followed, lifted us, and hurled us forward, clear. We gained new headway from the wind and shot ahead through a cauldron of white surf.

We struck again, were lifted by a bigger sea, carried two fathoms on its crest—and dropped so viciously that every fibre of the boat was strained. The stern swung round and we lay grounded, broadside to the wind and sea.

A squall struck, throwing us on our beam ends: in the wild tumult of the sea and wind we lowered sail and anchored.

We lay a quarter of a mile from shore. It was almost dark, and the falling tide soon left us in the very midst of breaking seas.

(5 8)

MOUNT SEYMOUR

It was the work of some minutes to get the spare anchor out of the hold and bolt its uncouth parts together. The mate in this emergency became again a miracle of energy and strength and prompt obedience. With the white seas curling over the skiff's gunwale, he rowed the heavy anchor with its dragging weight of chain to windward, and at the chain's length dropped it. Then, taking advantage of every lift of the larger seas, we strained to draw the bow into the wind. Time and again without avail we pulled the anchor through the yielding sandy bottom, hove it aboard, replaced it in the skiff, and the mate carried it to sea again. The bow stuck fast. Finally, after an hour of exhausting labor, we worked the boat's stern into the wind and, with both anchors at their chain's and cable's lengths to windward, held her so, and went below to await the tide or dissolution.

Battening the companionway doors against the wind and the heavy seas that now and then boarded the stern, we rekindled the fire, that had burned out during our preoccupation, and settled down grimly to enjoy what dismal comfort was to be had.

Being, because of his youth and his wide experience of calamity, the more hopeful of us two, the mate was in this hour of misfortune the more dejected. The emotions trace a circle, with their cause as center and the radius the measure of disaster. While he sat overwhelmed by thought of the damage that our ship must suffer, I, with less hope, had already seen her thrown upon the shore, a total wreck. I had accepted this

(59)

as an inevitable and therefore a finished episode. I had seen us stranded there—without a boat, to be sure, but quite alive and well. I had planned what we should save and, all in one moment of imagination, visioned our triumphant passage of the mountains southward. Out of the very all-eliminating completeness of disaster rose the sun upon a clean, new world. I laughed to see the mate so haggard and dispirited.

"Roll on, thou deep and dark blue ocean, roll!" I declaimed in tragically moving tones. And when, with lowered voice and the slow rhythm of the pendulum of destiny, I spoke these lines:

"He sinks into thy depths with bubbling groan,
Without a grave, unknelled, uncoffined and unknown."

the deep and bitter cup of the mate's misery bubbled over; he laughed. Nature, for both of us, had overdone its drama.

I remember years ago, when my older children were very little and we were all living in a tiny, one-room, abandoned schoolhouse in the Middle West, that they heard there, for the first time, thunder: and it was thunder so terrific that it seemed like a concussion of the universe about the little shell that held us. And the children were frightened. So we gave them each a tin pan and a heavy kitchen spoon.

"Take these," we said, "and when it thunders beat as hard as you can on the pans and see if you can make a bigger noise than the thunder. It's a game."

They did make a bigger noise, and loved it; and therewith ended forever the terrors of thunder.

No sound of nature could be more gruesomely harassing than that intermittent grinding, gnashing, thumping, creaking, groaning of our forlorn ship as she rolled and pounded in that sea. So I got out my beautiful, beloved silver flute and played upon it; and if It had never before imposed a mood of peace upon one human spirit— and that is possible—that day, by the incongruousness of its plaintive notes amid those sounds of wreck, it did.

Then, lo! as if the forces of destruction had grown discouraged in the face of our impressive nonchalance, the tides of the sea and of fortune turned to favor us. Instead of lifting on the crests of waves we floated free, and only pounded in the hollows.

With new energy and strength we went to work to improve our position, and in an hour's time, by pulling the vessel out to the anchors and carrying the anchors alternately out to sea, we reached a safe depth to lie in. It was an extremely rough and uncomfortable berth, but in the total darkness of that night it was out of the question to hoist canvas and look for another. Utterly exhausted, we turned in.

CHAPTER IX

FLAMES AND DESTRUCTION

AFTER a restless night we were about at dawn, to find that the wind and sea
had moderated. It was again low tide and the calmer water revealed to
us the devious course of the true channel. It was decided that while I
kept the appointment with Gómez to go with him to Lago Fognano,
the mate should take the boat up the river and anchor her there, and proceed alone
on the following day to join me at the lake.

Gómez appeared at six o'clock riding along the shore and leading another horse.
"Splendid!" I thought, "here's where I ride." But the horse carried a pack saddle,
which the owner showed no inclination to remove. And after a most friendly, smiling
greeting, my guide started up the valley at a brisk pace that kept me jogging at the
horse's tail.

There can be little conversation between men who have scarcely ten words in
common. However, out of my feelings over the near disaster of the night before I
managed to tell Gómez that he might have instructed us about the passage.

"Yes, it is very bad," he said, and laughed maliciously. "You have no gun!" he
remarked presently, in astonishment that I was weaponless. "Must have gun. Very
bad men around here; and wild cattle, very bad." He carried a Winchester slung over
his shoulder and the customary large heavy knife on his hip.

The trail followed the south bank of the river. After crossing the broad green
pasture plain we began the ascent of the valley. The ground was uneven and difficult.
Small streams and tracts of bog obstructed us and finally forced my guide to dismount.
The horses became an encumbrance and floundered miserably, at times getting mired
to their bellies. You hardly walk, you flounder in the bog. Its substance is like satu-

(61)

rated sponge, it swallows up your steps, it wearies you and wets you through. Still we made good time.

Before three hours we had mounted several hundred feet, and, turning, saw the sound behind us like a map, with little foam-encircled islands on its surface and the white waves showing like tiny flowers in a dark blue meadow. And under the enchantment of that distance and the clear beauty of the day the memory of the near-to terrors of the sea appeared illusion. No wonder that in the far-off sight of God nothing should matter.

Presently, on reaching dry soil and the shelter of a grove of trees, we stopped for rest. We warmed ourselves beside a fire and ate a refreshment of chocolate that I had brought. Then, leaving the horses, we proceeded through the woods.

Through occasional openings in the forest the lake was now revealed below us. That spurred us on; and the dry soil and the smooth creature-trodden paths made our swift pace a pleasure.

Suddenly a shot sounded from the lake, and across a sunlit clearing just in front of us passed a flash of white and gold, and the swift rush of moving bodies. We reached the open space. There paused a moment and then leaped away a herd of the most graceful deerlike creatures, gleaming white and cream, so beautiful: guanacos. They arched their swanlike necks and leapt the fallen trunks and bounded toward the mountain side. One stopped and turned with timid curiosity and looked at us; and then took sudden fright, and he was gone.

And in that spot, where there had been the beauty of those living things, was but the dull wilderness again, with hoarse men's voices sounding from the lake, and Gómez firing futilely at the deserted mountain side. Hidden among the mountains of Tierra del Fuego, sheltered by their barriers against the cold winds of the south and kept inviolate against the devastations of human enterprise, lies Lake Fognano: scarcely a hundred men can ever have beheld it.

I stood upon a little grassy knoll, and from my feet far eastward stretched the lake, unbroken to its own horizon: above that line the peaks of mountains sixty miles away marked its far end. It was midday and the warm sun shone on us from the cloudless north. Calm and silent was that hour but for the faintest far-off roaring of the west wind in the forests of the mountain sides. Waves of silver swept over the grass lands; silver and gold were the wild marshes and the glistening shore, blue was the lake and tender green the budding forest tops; and the high mountain peaks stood dazzling white against the profound deeps of space. There are moments in the experience of beauty whose ecstasy transcends all memory or vision of happiness, so that their unrelated present stands complete as an immeasurable stellar lifetime.

A shout shattered the silence. Turning, I saw a big fellow, armed with a rifle and belted about with cartridges, striding toward me.

"Where are they? Where'd they go?" he yelled. "God, look!"

(62)

GUANACO PASTURE

And dropping on one knee he took careful aim at a point high up the mountain side, and fired. Making their way across an open knoll were three or four guanacos.

The hunter fired to his feverish heart's content; then, shouting that he'd struck one, went tearing up the mountain side. There was a shouting of men, a firing of guns, a barking of dogs, the bedlam of a hunter's carnival—fainter and farther off, till men and dogs were lost to sight and hearing in the tangled ravines of the wild slopes. And as at last after a long time they struggled back again, there could be seen high up the mountain, close to the lower patches of the snow that crowned it, the same guanacos daintily on their upward way, all unconcerned. And so, the great hunt being over, the hunter came and greeted me and shook my hand.

He was a big, hearty, red-faced boisterous fellow, this German, Mulach, generous and kind; and his joy at meeting with a stranger who would be his guest was like a child's in its impulsiveness. One cannot know the friendliness and warmth of human beings but through the privilege of an encounter in the wilderness. So, parting from my saintly guide, I set out with the excommunicated Mulach and his Chilean gaucho, Juan, for the German's farm across the lake, the Estancia Isabel.

(63)

We embarked in a crazy flat-bottomed rowboat, on which, a good breeze having sprung up, we rigged a square sail of a patch of canvas. An hour's sailing brought us to the northern shore a few miles up the lake. Here in a little creek we beached the boat and started for the house that stood half hidden by a grove of trees. A pretty, red-cheeked, blue-eyed, sweet-voiced little boy came running gleefully to meet his father. The wife stood on the threshold and greeted us with eager joy; and with the spirit of a real homecoming we stamped into the warm kitchen. In almost no time we are feasting our hungry bellies on delicious currant bread and tea.

"This," says our host, mumbling through a mouthful, "is free and easy place. Make yourself at home and stay as long as you can."

And there we did stay, held for days and weeks by circumstance, until the very acceptance of our host's kindness and of the care-free ease and comfort of the daily life they offered us became a reproach to us.

The Estancia Isabel is, with the exception of the Silecian and Indian settlements at the extreme eastern end, the only inhabited spot on Lake Fognano. It occupies an extent of about ten miles of the comparatively flat meadow and timberland that borders the northwestern end of the lake; but the little enterprise had encountered natural obstacles so incommensurable with the limited capital and pioneering genius behind it that it appeared scarcely to have scarred the pristine order of the region.

The main building of the farm was the dwelling house, a barracklike structure built of pit-sawn boards, comprising four rooms that opened onto a covered veranda. There were, besides, a pigsty, a henhouse, a ramshackle shed or two, a corral, a sheep dip. There were a stump-cluttered, carcass-littered, sodden barnyard, a fenced garden, a surrounding tract of half-burnt forest with huge surviving trees towering over a wilderness of fallen trunks and branches. There were the miles of fenced-in "camp," of woods and bog with only here and there a bit of clear dry pasture land, and beyond this "camp" the untrodden forests of the mountain side.

On the Estancia Isabel lived Mulach and his wife and child, and two Chileños. There were three pigs, a few hens, six horses and as many head of cattle. It was spring and the German had but recently arrived to supersede a Chilean manager.

But in what Mulach had already undertaken or accomplished appeared that genius for pioneering which has made the German residents of Chile the most potent force in the country's development. His was a nature to be kindled into a frenzy of activity by the very chaos of disorder into which he had fallen; and the profusion of the unclaimed resources of that wilderness stimulated his vision of accomplishment and roused him to destructive energy against the obstacles of nature that thwarted it. He saw in that wild forest land broad cultivated fields, which in the sun-warmed, sheltered valley of the lake would yield rich crops of grain. He saw fat sheep and cattle browsing on its fertile pastures. He saw the mountain streams converted into power, the forest into lumber, the lumber into barns and houses. He saw the region populous

MOUNTAIN AT FOOT OF FOGNANO

and prospering with folk whose freedom was the flower of their isolation there.

And he was not only a dreamer. He plunged into the work of destruction with a madman's frenzy, ripping, tearing, hacking at the jungle, piling high the brush and burning it, till out of the chaos that destruction first achieved emerged the order of man's cultivation.

One day at evening twilight he kindled a great accumulation of rubbish that lay on the border of the forest near the farmyard clearing. A strong wind was blowing; within ten minutes a full acre was ablaze. The fire leapt the tallest growing trees, and these flamed to the sky like burning oil tanks. The whole region of the ancient forest encumbered with fallen trunks and inflammable brush, and dry bogs and meadows of long grass, lay in the fire's path as fuel for its flames; the stock, the sheep, the bridge, the pasture fences, everything above the ground to no one knew what limits to the east was threatened with destruction. The sense of imminent disaster, the furnace heat, the roaring of the flames and their lurid glare in the oncoming darkness, struck terror in us. The German rushed about in wild excitement, a demon figure against the flames.

"It's going, isn't it? The whole damned thing!" he shouted.

Together we circled through the forest. Only the flames now lit the darkness there, throwing their lurid light far down the gloomy aisles. Small fires were starting all about us.

(65)

LAKE FOGNANO

"Nothing to be done," said the German hopelessly; and suddenly, right there in the fire's track, in heat almost too great to bear, he began, with sentiment that is only German, gathering sprays of the orange-flowered califata bush for a bouquet—"before they burn," he said.

The fate of the farm and the wilderness having passed into the control of destiny, we went to supper and ate with almost unconcern.

The flames raged fiercely for three hours. They swept through the dry rubbish of the nearest clearings, destroyed some lengths of timber fence, penetrated a distance into the living forest; and then in struggle with the dampness there miraculously died.

It had been arranged that the mate should meet me at the lake on the day following my coming there, and signal his arrival across the water by kindling the dry grass on the promontory. Accordingly, to combine a morning of sport with the chore of ferrying, I embarked after breakfast with Mulach and Juan and crossed the lake to an extensive plain that lay on the southern shore a few miles below our point of rendezvous. The plain appeared to Mulach not only a likely place for guanacos but promising land for the extension of the farm pasturage.

The day was fair, and the inevitable west wind was at that hour too light to impede our progress with the oars. While still far distant from the spot for which we headed, guanacos were to be discerned on the wild meadows bordering the shore; and as we neared the land several came down onto the sandy beach and watched us curiously. Our close approach at last alarmed them all but one whose eager interest kept him lingering, until, at the grounding of the boat, he took sudden fright and like a flash leaped into the covert and vanished. The hunters followed after him, and for an hour I was left alone.

I wandered out upon a point of firm dry land that lay between the lake and an extensive marsh. Here was a true wilderness—untouched by man, and yet so beautifully cleared beneath its grove of slender trees, with lawns of short-cropped grass and smooth-trodden paths, that it was like a park. It was sheltered there and warm, and so quiet that you heard the lapping of the wavelets on the beach. But the wild animals whose place it was had fled—and one was sadly conscious of intrusion.

Meanwhile the hunt went on, and my Franciscan reverie was punctuated by the sound of shots that marked the hunter's progress. The Chileño presently returned with the proud air of a conqueror to conduct me to an animal that he had bagged.

Our path lay through a forest of lofty southern evergreen—the coigue, and the so-called oak, or roblé. It was a vaulted dense-roofed forest, dark and cool within, clean floored and dry and softly carpeted with grass and moss; and, leading everywhere and nowhere were the smooth guanacos' paths. It was the Paradise of the guanacos; and the gentle creatures by centuries of unmolested living there had impressed upon the wilderness the tranquillity of their own natures.

We came to a broad, swift-flowing, sunlight-flooded river where the brown pebbles glistened like precious stones through the limpid water, and the califata drooped its flowering branches in the stream.

"There!" said the Chileño.

In the shoal water against the far bank of the stream crouched a wounded guanaco. It held its long neck erect and looked at us, quietly. The Chileño threw a stone that thumped its ribs. It struggled desperately to climb the bank, sank back, and then again looked at us quietly. I told the fellow to shoot it. The bullet struck behind the ear. The guanaco leaped again, fell back. The long, swanlike neck slowly arched toward the stream. The mouth, touching the water, tried to drink. The arched neck dropped—and a great flood of crimson blood flowed from the mouth and dyed the river red.

The German appeared, having shot another two miles up the stream; and for hours the wilderness was rent with shouting and splashing and plunging and crashing as we worked to navigate the carcasses through the shoals and rapids and snaring obstructions of the current of the lake. And as we left the dry meadows we fired them behind us, till the smoke of huge conflagration hung over everything; so that our retreat with flames and corpses partook of the glory of a military progress.

(67)

At the lake the bedraggled carcasses were pulled ashore; and, with the flushed heroes posing over them against the tranquil distant mountains and the sky, I photographed that sportsman's tableau.

But hours of daylight still remained and, although no smoke of the mate's signal fire had met our watchfulness, we loaded the guanacos into the boat and began laboriously to row down the lake toward the place of rendezvous. The boat was heavy laden and the wind was strong, and it was near sundown when, in the lee of the appointed promontory, we went ashore to rest.

We sat on a sheltered spur of the hillside with the warm sun shining on our backs. Below us in the shadow of the hill was the smooth crescent beach with our boat drawn up on it. The mountains were golden under the westering sun and on the blue lake now lay the peacefulness of evening. For a long time we sat there without speaking, for the spell of that infinite serenity was over us: and I repeated quietly to Mulach the sonnet which is the breath of that same cosmic peacefulness that there embraced us.

> "*Returning home at evening, with an ear*
> *Catching the notes of Philomel—an eye*
> *Watching the sailing cloudlet's bright career,*
> *He mourns that day so soon has glided by:*
> *E'en like the passage of an angel's tear*
> *That falls through the clear ether silently.*"

Suddenly there sounded a breaking twig in the thicket near us. Both men sprang for their guns and followed it. A moment passed, and then two shots were fired almost simultaneously. There were shouts and a crashing of the underbrush. The hideous thing was irresistible, and, cursing them, I followed.

Down at the bottom of a dark depression in a dense and beautiful canelo grove, among the moss-grown roots and fallen trunks, was the Chileño astride the fallen but still living guanaco. With the man's arms tight around its neck it struggled frantically to rise. They tied a lasso to one of its hind legs, and the animal, freed of the man's weight, got upon its feet and leaped—and fell again.

A foreleg had been shattered by the bullet. Again it struggled and plunged headlong with wild attempts at freedom, and would have gained it but that the lasso pulled it back. Thus, desperately floundering, they drove it toward the shore and to the very boat itself. Out in the clear, cool daylight on the beach it fell exhausted. Holding its long neck erect, it looked furtively about with dark, round eyes that still seemed unalarmed.

The Chileño straddled it; and while with mock tenderness he took its head caressingly against his cheek, he carefully placed his knife point at the base of the throat and drove it home. Out of the belly they took a baby one, well grown.

We dumped the two animals into the boat, set fire to the grass of the hillside and to the green canelo grove, seated ourselves as best we could on top of the warm carcasses, and, with the boat loaded to the gunwale, rowed cautiously away.

Twilight descended as we crossed. But long after the mountain bases and the lowlands were in shadow the smoke of burning meadows and forests mounted up into the golden light.

CHAPTER X

THE MATE'S ADVENTURE

THE day following the hunt, hoping to rest my land-weary sea legs, I hobbled off into the concealment of the woods to escape my host's relentless energy and persecuting kindness—only at last to be sought out and dragged on wearying excursions over the trackless bog and tangled jungle of the camp. We watched all day in vain for the smoke of the mate's signal fire, and with evening came anxiety as to what had befallen him.

The following morning, as early as the slothful habits of the Chileños would permit, I set out on horseback with Juan, decidedly the more agreeable of the temperamental pair, to find fresh horses on the range in order that we might the next day ride down to the port. The horse and cattle range is the unfenced wilderness, and a round-up may be the work of an hour or a day or a week, as luck shall determine.

Our way first lay along the shore. It was a blue day and a windy one. The surf broke on the shingle and its icy spray flew over us and wet and chilled us to the marrow. We crossed the border line of Chile and rode far into Argentina, watching continually for fresh horse tracks.

Found at last, they led us through wild wastes of bog and marsh, in which our horses floundered to the belly; and they led through bramble thickets and through dense and tangled copses of stunted trees; they traversed tracts of noble forest following the smooth paths of the guanaco. Deep in the forest in a verdant glade we found

(70)

the horses. Juan with the lasso secured three. We led them to the lake; there, driving them before us, we galloped madly home.

It was five o'clock. Mrs. Mulach, a plain little Englishwoman, indefatigably active, neat, irritable, kind and generous, was preparing supper. The rapid clatter of her little steps sounded on the wooden floor as she raced about the narrow circuit of her destiny —the stove, the table, the meat block and the flour bin.

The familiar steam of the eternal mutton soup was wafted on the air.

"Supper!" roared Mulach, coming to the door.

The port of Estancia Isabel is the northern of the two bays at the head of Admiralty Sound, and is known as Jackson Bay. A rough trail had been laid out through the valley north of the Mount Hope range, and over those twelve difficult miles passed all the estancia's traffic with the outside world. With Juan as my guide, I set out on the following morning for the port, leading a spare horse for the mate. The track was extremely rough, and the occasional bridges of corduroy were either in such poor repair or so isolated in the churned bog of their approach that they had rather to be avoided than made use of. In traversing bog it is the judgment of the horse that is most to be relied upon. The little native animals have a real instinct for safe footing, and will often stop and refuse to venture upon perilous spots that to the human eye appear quite dry and firm. And in the forest they have equal assurance; threading their way however swiftly through the mazes of young-growth timber they never misjudge what they can leap or pass beneath or through; while at the same time, by their utter disregard of the rider's proportions, they threaten him with the fate of Absalom.

We got no glimpse of the port nor of Admiralty Sound until we had covered three-quarters of the distance. For some miles the trail had crept up the mountain side, leaving the valley gradually below it on the right.

A steep hill confronted us with its edge cut sharp against the sky as if beyond it there were nothing. The trail led over it. With the suddenness of our arrival on the summit, wild as the biting wind that greeted us, the whole vast marvel of the sound displayed itself.

The day was clouded, and the wind-swept water gleamed like fluid metal between the far-receding, iron-dark mountain walls that enclosed it; and against the lurid brightness of the west stood the steel-blue peaks of Dawson Island.

At a reckless trot we descended the steep, stony trail to the plain of the port. On that arid, treeless flat the wind blew with new violence accumulated from the flanking mountain sides. Scarcely above the reach of the tide on the smooth sand beach of the bay stood a rough cabin that served as a lodging for the men of the Estancia Isabel on their occasional visits to the port; so weathered was it by the wind-blown spray and drifting sand that it seemed a part of that cast-up mess of refuse from the sea in which it stood.

(71)

ADMIRALTY SOUND FROM THE HEAD

   In the tangled meadow a short stone's throw from the cabin stood a wooden cross that marked the grave of one whom the dreary solitude of the place had driven to suicide. Along the beach and seaward over the broad shoals of the bay thundered everlastingly the surf, adding the sound of desolation to that picture of it.

   After a refreshment of hot coffee and bread, we set out upon the long, slow climb around the face of Mount Hope, to arrive at the southern bay. Following a precipitous ascent up wooded steeps, we attained the relatively level plain of a spur of the mountain. Here again, between broad ledges of rock, was bog, and the dwarfed trees that almost lay upon the ground were evidence of the prevailing violence of the western winds that raked it.

   Since the day following my arrival at the lake I had struggled with an anxiety about the safety of the *Kathleen* that only my enforced powerlessness to act had kept in philosophical control. Now, however, as every height we reached and every promontory that we turned held out the hope of a view of the other bay and a disclosure of what disaster to my boat had kept the mate from joining me, I became a helpless prey to the worst anxieties, and steeled myself to bear the reality of that picture of a wreck-strewn shore which my imagination formed. As successive points of promise were reached and passed only to confront us with new barriers, our eager pace was quickened to the limit of my endurance. I tired; fatigue and repeated disappointments let my dark forebodings fix themselves upon me with the strength of certainty.

Then, suddenly, around the shoulder of a headland that our path encircled, appeared the bay! Not all of it. First came to view the far-off southern end of the long shore; smooth, clean, unblemished sand it was, and the dark sea was breaking in long rollers on it. As we advanced the even drama of that strand deployed itself with the serene, sustained and cumulative tension of great art. And as its curve swept toward us the enlarging volume of the roar of breakers mounted to our ears.

Then from that shore and from a hundred reefs and islands sheer below us the full thunder of the sea expanded. Our eyes took in the scene. There lay the bay with not a mark upon its long, clear beach; there was the river's mouth with the clear current flowing unobstructed through; and there, in the sheltered basin that the broadening river made behind the dunes, rode the tiny *Kathleen*, safe at anchor. And no eyes ever met a sight more grateful.

How we raced down the intervening half mile to the boat and riotously hailed the mate to ferry us aboard is needless to be told. Seated, presently, in the warm cabin over tea, he related his adventures.

At high tide of the day that I departed for the lake he weighed anchor and, without taking the anchor on board, sailed around into the channel of the river and gained its mouth. Here he encountered a strong current, but with a fair wind he passed slowly and safely through. He anchored in the lagoon some distance below the bridge.

The following morning, just at daybreak, he was awakened by the grounding of the boat. It proved that the strong river current had dragged the anchor through the yielding pebble bottom. He shifted it to a sandy point downstream, burying it three feet in the sand, and secured two stern lines to the bridge. Nevertheless, the river current was of such strength, and subject to such uncertain variations by the influence of the tide, that he postponed starting for the lake until another day.

The second day, however, ushered in the wind as a new force to harass the boat at her unstable anchorage. But in spite of violent squalls the anchor held, and the day passed without untoward happening. The mate was uneasy and lay down that night without undressing. The wind increased to a gale. At one o'clock the flood tide invaded the river to where the *Kathleen* lay, and dissipating the opposing force of the current, gave the boat into the power of the wind. The anchor that lay to the windward was torn free: with the crash of the boat against the bridge the mate awoke.

From that hour, until at four ebb tide relieved him, the mate sat braced upon the bridge and kept the boat away; and the measure of his strength and endurance is to be found in that he succeeded where the anchor failed.

Trouble of this sort was, however, at an end. The *Kathleen's* bow was held down-

BRIDGE ACROSS AZAPARDO RIVER

stream by two anchors locked into the roots of trees, and the stern moored to the bridge.

Juan returned that evening to the port. Next morning, laden with such quantity of table luxuries as we could carry (Mrs. Mulach "loved pickles"), we joined him there, and pursued an uneventful journey homeward to the farm.

Mulach's welcome was the heartiest; and, as if in celebration of our return, he kindled a towering brush heap. We sat around it in the darkness and watched the sparks mount up and mingle with the stars. It was so utterly and beautifully peaceful in that place that there crept over me a sense of the profound familiarity of the environment, as if it were and ever had been home. And then I felt the marvel of that mood's annihilation of the *facts* of seven thousand intervening miles and months of journeying, by which those facts of time and space became illusion, and the spirit's vision revealed itself as the truth.

Under the spell of those hot dragon-tongues of flame that lapped the night we might have lain for hours watching the fire as a symbol of the mind consume the heaped-up roots and trunks of the material world, and at last through the very ecstasy of peace have beheld within ourselves an unfolding of the deeper beauties of the spirit's universe. That was not to be. Mulach's wild energy kept him impervious to dreams. He sprang about tearing up roots; and, like a demon, he forever piled more trash upon the flames.

Mulach's relentlessness had almost worn me out, and yet the great test of our endurance was before us. For days he had talked of an expedition—to which, for the huge importance that was attached to it and the verbal preparation that was made, I shall devote a chapter.

CHAPTER XI

THE GREAT EXPEDITION

WE were to find a passage through the lofty mountain ranges that lay to the north of the Estancia Isabel, out to the settled region that from there stretched northward to the Strait, and eastward to the Rio Grande. It was important, for many reasons, that a track of communication be established here. And it seemed to Mulach opportune and to us attractive—albeit a little terrifying because of that tireless energy of our guide—to go upon this expedition while we were there.

Almost with dawn of that momentous day Willie and I arose and dressed. We waited hours before the household stirred. With breakfast over we began to pack. The expedition was to go afoot and take a horse to carry the supplies. We were to spend one night at least.

"What shall I take?" I asked our chief.

"Nothing! We'll show you how to do it here. A great big fire; lie down in front of it. Don't need a thing. Blankets? No: don't need 'em. A tent? No: don't bring yours. I have a big one. Room enough for all of us if it rains."

I had a number of simple camp conveniences that I timidly suggested taking, but was told we couldn't bother with such stuff. However, a kettle of mine was accepted and into this I smuggled some evaporated soup and a nest of four drinking cups instead of one, which Mulach had said would be enough for four people. Willie and I exchanged looks and let things take their course. Somehow, when the horse stood ready for the march it carried a great number of bales and rolls.

We started. Out past the last bounds of the farm into the untrodden forest we went, climbing an easy ascent toward the mountain divide that we had chosen to penetrate.

(76)

I, with my compass, led the party, choosing the path and clearing it a little of dead stuff. Mulach and Juan came next, Juan with a machete and Mulach with a meat cleaver. They blazed and hacked and cleared the path of the obstructing saplings for Willie and the horse, who followed last. It was my good fortune over a part of our way to find a smooth guanaco trail, which I so much improved by throwing out dead limbs and branches that the others, impressed and astonished by its width and beauty, with one accord named the trail Camino Kent—by which name, whatever posterity may choose to call it, it shall always live in my memory.

But the forest was dry and open and, despite the extensive cutting and blazing of our pioneers, we made good progress, and found ourselves by early afternoon high on one mountain side within the pass itself, and the other mountain side in view across the gorge of a stream. We stopped for a meal. Juan left on a fruitless search for guanacos, while Mulach roasted mutton on a wooden spit, and I made tea.

From here on our path became more difficult. The mountain side was steep and thickly grown with small trees. We soon came to patches of snow that the horse found difficulty in crossing. As we advanced the patches became fields of snow, waist deep in spots, and dwarfed trees, bent and twisted by the wind, grew like entanglements across our path. Below us ran the torrent between steep, thickly wooded banks, and above us, not three hundred yards away, the timber line offered a trail more steep, undoubtedly, but free at least of trees.

I went ahead to try it there, climbing through such a densely matted growth of dwarfed trees, crawling in their tops, plunging into drifts about their roots and stems, that I wondered if the horse could ever be brought to follow; yet he was. We reached the timber line and tracked through mountain moss and low bushes, occasionally crossing slides of slaty stone or, in the depressions, drifts of snow. The mountain sides rose steeply over us with jagged snow-patched peaks against the zenith sky; and far below us over the green forest tops of the valley lay the blue lake, and, still beyond, the snow-capped mountain barrier whose southern slope descended to the sea.

We reached an eminence from which appeared the full extent of the pass we were attempting. It was quite closed by a mountain as lofty as those on either side of us, presenting only the possibility of a winding passage to the eastward. The valley of our stream terminated in a grassy flat enclosed by hills. It was winter. The cold blue shadows of late afternoon had settled over the scene but for where the low sun shot brilliant shafts of light between the peaks and lit the high rim of our pass.

We led the horse down the shaly incline, across a deep snow field out onto the river meadow and there left him to graze. Willie, free of his charge, rushed on ahead; and, as Mulach and I toiled over the snow to that side at which a passage might be found we saw him, a tiny black figure on the vast expanse of snow, mounting up to where the steep mountain faces closed the path.

(77)

NEAR THE TIMBER LINE

Somehow, thanks to the hard training of the past few days and to the stimulating, thrilling splendour of the mountain country we had reached, I felt as strong and fresh as if the day were just beginning. There's a distracting joy in new discovery, fed by the faith one has that every height ascended will reveal a wonderland.

And so I said to Mulach, "We'll go on! We'll send Juan back home with the horse, and then see if there isn't a way through here."

But Mulach, strangely, wouldn't.

"Give me the gun," I urged, "or what's left of the mutton. Nothing more. The mate and I will find your pass. And we'll go clear around and come back by some other way!"

"No, no," he repeated stubbornly, "we must all stick together."

Still, we climbed to the highest point of the pass itself, a rounded field of snow of unknown depth. And from that top we looked into an immense ravine, another valley, leading southward back to the lake again, and northward into mountains where its course was hid from view. This valley was enclosed between immense, steep mountain sides of unbroken form that, clothed in sombre forest, descended to their very meeting in the darkness of a narrow gorge. Northward, around a mountain spur the golden evening light streamed into it and somehow gave the promise of green plains and pastures with the glint of distant settlements.

(78)

"Come on," I cried, for Mulach was lagging, "we'll travel until dark and find the valley."

For a moment I won him. Together we started down the snowy slope. We sank in to our knees. A hundred yards or so we went—then Mulach stopped.

"No, we'll go back," he snapped.

Then like a flash of light it came to me that he was tired! If I'd been almost dead I'd not have told him so, it was so sweet to have revenge for those hot, miserable miles he'd dragged me through the marsh and bog and river bed to get his dead guanaco. I followed his retreating homeward steps exuberantly urging him to climb the slopes. He only was more set on getting home again—or back to camp. He'd take the horse, he said, and travel down a way to where we'd had our lunch and there prepare things for the night. So, for a while, we parted, and I ascended the ridge of the mountain that lay between the two valleys. I was on its northern slope where it was free of snow. Rich, green and russet moss and heather grew where the slides of shale had not covered or swept away the soil. It was not a difficult climb, except a few feet of steep, sharp-edged rock that had to be scaled in order to reach the summit of the ridge itself. Once there, on what had seemed, as I climbed up, to be the highest peak of the mountain, I was confronted by a succession of similar knobs of the same elevation or higher; but the hour was too late to continue.

The sun shone from over the westward range and it was warm. I sat down in a soft bed of moss, lighted my pipe, and, breathing deep contentment, surveyed the scene. Far off lay the great blue lake with the west wind trailing purple cloud shadows like veils across it; lay the thick forested slopes and level lands—light green with budding foliage and flooded with the sunshine of late afternoon. And above the summer landscape of the valley, thirty miles away in the blue haze of the south, stood the serrated peaks of the Darwin mountains in eternal winter. Straight down below me I saw the mate and Mulach and the horse, three tiny figures threading their way down the valley of the stream; and I saw Juan, alone, climbing the snow slope toward the northwest.

The colors of the rocks and minute vegetation of my peak resembled in depth and brilliance the bottom of a rocky tide-pool by the sea; and the texture of the mosses was as rich and varied as ecclesiastical embroidery.

Sitting there in lofty solitude, it occurred to me that I was the first man ever to have scaled that peak. And, since the mountain, being of no particular importance or prominence, had never been named, I christened it, for reasons of most tender sentiment, Mount Barbara.

But it was getting late—and cold, and all my companions were long gone out of sight. I hurried down the mountain side, sliding down the slopes of shale, running and jumping into moss beds, coasting down toboggan slides of snow. Jubilantly I marched along the river valley singing "John Brown's Body."

(79)

Dusk had descended as I entered the forest and here it soon deepened to a light-and-shadowless obscurity. "It will be nice," it kept occurring to me, "to arrive at the camp they have made, to rest and dry myself before the great log fire. Maybe the supper is cooked. By God! that will taste fine!" And with appetite as a spur I broke into a run.

I reached the appointed place and it was deserted, nor were there any tracks to show they had passed that way. I pursued my course, holloing as I went, but getting no response.

The twilight in those latitudes is long. I could see to travel and I raised my pace against the threat of darkness. I shouted—and the echo of my own voice answered. A mile more and I had almost reached the limit of my patience, and in disgust and fury planned to settle for the night, alone. It was then that, far away, I heard an answering call.

In the thickest of the woods, a great distance from the proper trail, I came upon them, the mate with the horse, and Mulach; not camped, nor even waiting, but there in the darkness plunging on blindly through the wilderness, with the German like a madman hacking with his cleaver, climbing, running, falling, staggering on, and the poor horse plunging in that darkness over logs and into pits. The party seemed to be in frantic flight.

"What's up?" I shouted, bursting upon them. Mulach stopped.

"Where's Juan?" he demanded.

I could have killed him.

He seemed in utter bewilderment. Whether in fear of the darkness or unstrung by fatigue, he had been rushing on with the one wild hope of reaching home that night. That he was leaving two of us behind without food, that the way was long, the night dark and the forest trackless, that he could never get the horse through that wilderness at night, had not occurred to him.

"What shall we do?" he asked nervously.

I told him we must camp.

For camp we needed water. We plunged down the slope with Mulach hacking the way and uttering frenzied cries for Juan to hear. There in the darkness of a swampy glade we saw the glimmer of a pool, and in the woods near by we camped. Willie's disgust with things was absolute.

He and I worked together and made the camp. We built a great fire for warmth and a little one for our kettle. We put water on to boil, cut boughs for a bed and built a shelter of boughs against the wind. Mulach! I don't know what he busied himself about. I found him starting to put up his tent on some logs and brush, took pity on him and chose a better site. Juan came; and such a length of idle conversation as ensued between master and man no gossip could exceed.

"First," Mulach said, "we change our socks." And so they did, sitting before the

(80)

HALF-CLEARED FOREST

great fire I had built for them, Mulach and Juan. They were like children, innocent of plan or order.

"Here you see," called over Mulach, "the difference between the South American and the North American way of cooking. You have a pot and we use none."

Meanwhile our soup was coming to a boil. When I served it to them the roast had not yet been put on.

"Shall we have the meat tonight or for breakfast?" Mulach asked us innocently. "It is a leg of mutton."

"We have it tonight," I said.

After the soup there was a long time of waiting. Mulach and Juan said they were not hungry—but they made away in the interim with almost all our small supply of bread. At last we served the coffee, and drank it. And maybe half an hour after that the mutton à la South America was removed from the fire and placed on its long spit, sticking in the ground between us. It was fine!

Bedtime came. Out of the bundles from the horse's back were taken a canvas poncho, a heavy homespun woolen poncho and a great broad robe of guanaco skins. All of these and the sheepskins from under the pack saddle were carried into the tent by Juan and a bed made of them. We watched in dumb astonishment. But when Mulach suddenly disappeared into the tent with a cheerful "good-night, there's room for one more inside if you want to come," the air was thick with our unspoken thoughts. In a few minutes, as we lay there on the ground beside our fire, we heard the master's well known, gentle snoring.

One miserable night is easily borne. We had no coats nor covering of any kind, and it was freezing cold. We laughed a bit at the absurdity of it. The mate slept now and again. I stoked the fire, welcoming for warmth's sake the need there was of roaming about in search of firewood. I'd stir up the fire and by its light roam into the woods and drag back fallen trunks and roots. Just before dawn I slept a little.

When I got up at daylight to put the kettle on, Juan came out of the tent and helped. Willie slept on like a child. He had edged up nearly into the flames. With breakfast ready we called Mulach. He came stumbling out still half asleep, rubbing his eyes to make them meet the light.

"Oh, what a night!" he moaned, "I didn't sleep a wink."

That was our chance. We told him we had slept *too* warm, that we'd been forced to strip off some of our clothing in the night. We boasted of the great hardihood of Americans, who always slept coverless upon the ground when camping.

"Sometimes," I told him, "when the snow is deep and it is blowing hard we build a barricade of ice against the wind—but blankets?—never."

We regained our trail of the day before and hurried home. Passing across wild meadows we kindled them. The smoke rose in dense volume into the sky, and the morning sun shone through it luridly. At home Mulach went straight to bed.

Through pride I wouldn't, but grew ever more boastful of the intrepidity of North Americans. One day and night had gained me an ascendancy that I never relinquished.

But somehow we liked Mulach even better after this. The "great expedition" was over. We had turned back without accomplishing what we'd set out so resolutely to do; we had found the limit of our guide's illimitable energy and the evaporation point of his morale. We had, after all, explored a man; and it had been my privilege to look with understanding vision, as from an eminence, over the dreary foreground screen of masculine intrepidness into the sweet plains of a childlike nature. That Mulach had slept with all the bedclothes was only the thoughtlessness of a tired man. He had been good-natured and docile, and that was everything. It was fortunate that his wife believed in him, and right that she adored him. And if ever in a cold night one needed covering, Mulach, if asked, would give it—to his last guanaco robe.

"How did it happen," we inquired of Juan, "that all those things were brought?"

"I brought them," he answered—and laughed. "I know him."

CHAPTER XII

WIND-BOUND

ALL this time it was the wind that held us captive to the hospitality of the farm. It had seemed futile, as long as it held contrary, to attempt to sail out of Admiralty Sound, or even to move our boat from the river to a suitable anchorage outside. Every morning first of all we ran down to the shore and scanned the water and the sky; and every night at bedtime we looked with the same anxious hope aloft, and speculated on what change of wind the dawn might bring. And every day and night—but for an hour's calm at twilight—the wind was west. We pinned our faith upon the changes of the moon—and waited.

At last the particular day drew near and we prepared to return to the port. It was the mate this time who rode with Juan to find the horses. They returned at nightfall, and the mate carried a young guanaco behind his saddle. The creature had been painfully mutilated by the hound that had caught it, but it was still alive. We locked it in the shed for the night. The next day it lay there still living but unable to rise; its long neck was held erect, and its gentle rabbitlike countenance was curiously unexpressive of the body's suffering. I placed the muzzle of a revolver against the base of the skull and fired. The head jerked about convulsively and fell motionless. I had killed my first guanaco.

Where two or three are the whole world, a parting is pathetic. We bade many sad farewells to our hostess, and then, loaded with gifts of butter and bread and mutton and skins, and accompanied by Mulach and Juan, rode off into the forest.

But for the usual flounderings in the bog the trip was uneventful—except that my horse, wallowing in a soft hillside, lost his balance and rolled over, to the grave peril, if not of me, of my cameras and the eggs that were strapped to the saddle. He lay

ABOVE JACKSON BAY

there for a moment helpless, braced between his back and the sloping ground with his forelegs kicking in the air. But we pulled him around and with a quick struggle he got up.

To our vast pride Mulach marvelled at the trimness of the *Kathleen*. He remained with us that night as our first night's guest. We stuffed him with dainties and tucked him warm into bed.

"Some day," I told him at breakfast, "you'll come to North America to see us. And then I'll take you camping in American style." And I narrated an adventure of sleeping almost naked on cakes of ice.

Then, with many a good wish and the hope that we should meet again, we said good-bye to that kind, impulsive, generous man.

And then the moon changed. That this betokened change of wind all weather bureaus, almanacs, ancient mariners, weather-beaten guides and trappers, all knowing prophets of the wind and weather are agreed. Reason demands it, and convenience, and the universal law of change. And we believed it with a faith that was fathered by a deep and ardent desire.

So, that night, while the darkness imposed its wonted and expectant hush upon the elements, we put all things on board in order and retired early to be up to sail at dawn.

(86)

The dawn was breathless; but in that breathlessness we read the portent of a change. We went ashore and loosed our anchors from the roots where they were buried, we made the stern lines ready to cast off; we went below and breakfasted—and waited. And then, ever so gently, came the wind, came in little gusts that rippled up the water: and that wind was west. By ten o'clock the sky was overclouded and the interminable west wind howled as if the defiance of all law and of our hopes had sharpened its ferocity.

And now again for days we lay there wind-raked at our anchorage. The ocean tide and river current swirled about us. Even in that landlocked place the swell beat in and rocked us heavily. We *couldn't* sail. And the discomfort of our cabin was only preferable to the raw, tempestuous out-of-doors. It must be said that there were hours or quarter-hours of such contrasted warmth and loveliness that summer seemed to smile. Then the sheep would leave their sheltered huddling in the woods and take their new-born lambs for stilted frolics on the broad pasture plain. But very soon the clouds would close again and hide the sun, and, in a storm of wind, white winter would come again and cover the mountains and the plain with snow.

In such days of confinement as those we endured at our anchorage in the Azapardo River, when the world was narrowed to the bounds of a boat's cabin, and adventure was reduced to the hazards of bread making and dish washing, one's diary becomes a record of introspective journeys rather than of action.

"It is now the third of November," reads the page, "almost full moon, and a rising tide. The glass stands at 29. The west wind rakes our anchorage with undiminished force, whistling and howling. The tide rip gurgles venomously against our hollow sides, the seas strike us and hurl spray fiercely over us. Our cable creaks. The boat is rolling heavily and trembling when the squalls strike. I am driven from my reverie to bed.

"It is not easy to go to sleep on such a night as I have just recorded. Now, from another day, I look back upon it. I lay there in my bed listening to the innumerable sounds, and feeling by my close contact with the boat's thin sides her trembling response to the wild forces of the sea and wind. Sleep seemed impossible—yet, suddenly, I slept; and with that sleep all memory of the causes of my waking anxiety vanished. Still, as I must believe from the fragments of dreams that have been spared me out of that oblivion, I was by sleep transported to a world of the imagination as tragically full of peril, more harassing and, to the mind, in every way as real as the frightening actuality. I carried into sleep no memory of the daylight world, yet out of sleep I bore the recollection of experiences so terrible and of desire so hopeless of fulfillment that the mood of night clung like a pall about my consciousness. Of man's two existences, by day and night, night dominates.

"One of the ancient Christian faith would piously attribute his dreamt anxieties to visitations of Satan. But, as a pagan on the quest of happiness, I perceive them to

(87)

be the warnings of a man's own spirit that he may not forsake friendship and love and hope to live at peace."

At last a day dawned overcast and calm and ominous of change. And then, toward noon, out of the pregnant stillness came—could we believe it!—a gentle east wind. With wild precipitation we weighed anchor and on the swift current of the river swept out through the narrow channel to the sound. We have a moment's memory of the friends we leave. "Farewell!" our hearts cry, "we are sailing westward!"

An hour had passed. Every ripple had vanished and the sound lay as a mirror to the mountains. The air was breathless and our sails hung slack. For hours it held like this, while, helpless on the tide, we drifted to and fro. Then came the wind: far to the west we saw the water darkening in its path. It struck in squalls. In a rising storm under a sky as black as nightfall we made Jackson Bay and, under the scant shelter of its northern shore, dropped anchor.

Again for days we were held at anchor by the wind that blew with almost unabating violence. Once, in a lull, where there was, we thought, some indication of a coming change, we hoisted sail and beat out of the bay. The sky was leaden overhead and strangely near; and in the west it was a pallid yellow. Then, while the glass fell, the day became as dark almost as night. With sudden divination of trouble we came about and ran for port again. We reached our anchorage with wild squalls howling at our heels.

While we made the most of our incarceration by expeditions over the surrounding country, finding in the rugged grandeur of the overhanging northern mountain range and in the green and quiet twilight of the groves beauties enough to have contented us, still we grew restless under inactivity. The mountains lost their splendour in our eyes, the wilderness its charm; the unrelenting fury of the wind enraged us. Down the long stretch of Admiralty Sound, between its mountain walls and cliffs, it blew with an accumulated violence; and if aloft it veered a few points off, the canyon walls deflected it and held it in the groove. And it was not a steady wind: moments of almost calm would be followed by outbursts of concentrated fury as the congested gale was released to fall upon us from the mountain faces.*

---

*Captain Willis of the missionary schooner *Allen Gardiner* wrote —July 2nd (1883?)—of a trip of 280 miles, from Ushuaia to Punta Arenas, that took 110 days.

"On the 30th, the wind went to the south, blew a gale, and veered to north. We anchored on the wind falling light and variable before dark, and got under way this morning. Now it is calm and we are drifting helplessly back again . . . . I venture to say that calms and light weather, in which we are nearly stationary, often continue long enough to make a passage to Sandy Point, anchoring every night. These are generally followed by bad weather, in which it is almost impossible and dangerous to go, while night work is out of the question. We are now about 110 miles from Ooshooia in 26 days.

"Had this gale caught us in the night we should have assuredly been lost, as it is impossible to see anything, and very small sail can be carried, and often lowered down for five or ten minutes at a time. Compass and lead and log are of no use in these narrow waters, and if the vessel was to drift on some of these places she is so sharp she would, in all possibility, fall over and fill, if she was not knocked to pieces, and it would be useless getting a boat out on a lee shore. This is acknowledged by all nations to be one of the most dangerous places in the known world."

JACKSON BAY

Our boat, moreover, was not adapted to fine sailing. She made leeway and was slow in coming about. So we were often discouraged by losing in stays all that we had gained by half an hour's sailing. The tides were swift; and while not strong enough to help us much against a wind of any violence could, when contrary, more than check our progress.

And of the moods of the days of waiting the diary is a record.

"November seventh. It is late at night as I begin to write. For two hours we have sat here in the darkness of the cabin. The firelight shines through the grate, casting a faint warm glow about the room. The wind blows in terrifying squalls upon us, howling, careening us—and then for a few minutes it is quite still. The boat rocks gently, the little waves gurgle pleasantly against the sides, the clock ticks loudly; there is no sound in the world besides. Then again, far off, the forests of the mountain side begin to roar—nearer comes the sound and louder. Suddenly the gurgling water and the ticking clock, the little sounds that were so loud, are lost as the wild uproar of the wind engulfs us.

"We sit in silence every night throughout the twilight. Often I play upon the flute, shutting my eyes to make the darkness darker; and my companion's head is

OUR ANCHORAGE, JACKSON BAY

bowed and resting on his hands. In these still hours the wisdom comes to us of knowing our profoundest needs.

"Then with fatigue the glamour of adventure wanes; and loneliness comes over us and the sense that we are destitute of all that has sustained our lives. We that have come so far and left so much then know, out of the poignant singleness of our desires, what in the confusion and abundance of life's offerings is best. But no one tells —so intimately close and dear is that desire. And when at last, suddenly in the darkness here, I ask my companion what one thing he desires most out of the whole world, tonight—he starts at the shattered silence, and, slowly emerging from far away to here, covers his thoughts and answers, 'A fair wind to carry us through Gabriel Channel.' "

However, there's an end to everything. "Mate," I said one dreary night as we turned in, "I need a new chapter for my book. Tomorrow we sail no matter what happens." And we did.

CHAPTER XIII

"THE NEW CHAPTER"

THE morning was overcast and there was a light uncertain breeze from the west. The barometer was normal, at 29.07. But these placid indications counted for nothing, in my judgment, against the prevailing changefulness of the weather.

"We'd better reef," I ventured.

"Not a bit of it!" cried my mad mate. "Reef when we have to."

And so, unreefed, we sailed, for from the beginning it had been our rule that the more incautious should prevail.

The mate had more courage, blinder courage, more careless, reckless, stubborn nerve, than any man that I have ever seen or heard of. He was gifted to maintain this undiluted by any lessons of experience. *He forgot yesterday.*

And he was closed against tomorrow. He was untroubled by imagination or by any doubt of the comprehensiveness and finality of the rules of practice he had learned. And that his knowledge of seamanship and navigation had been acquired in the sailing of big ships on the open sea only made him contemptuous of the temperament of narrow waters and of little boats, and of the counsel of men whose experience was limited to these.

His rule of sailing and of life was contained in the old sailing-days expression, "carry on"; and if some day, bearing full sail on sea or land, he doesn't founder— then there's a special providence over the folly of men.

Once, long ago, I had said to him, "The thing is not to carry sail, but to get there." I had let it go at that and not concerned myself again—for after all it was an adventure.

(91)

ADMIRALTY SOUND I

We were an hour beating out of the cove. The entrance is narrow and on one side beset with islands; and the tide was against us. And in that hour's time the breeze died out and it grew ominously dark. Then the breeze freshened, blackening the water as it came. It takes no time to make a sea; whitecaps were flying and the spray broke over us. The barometer had dropped to 28.80.

The northern coast of Admiralty Sound is an immense sheer mountain wall of rock. Between its towered and buttressed summits the glaciers hang suspended, and the water of their melting snows pours in cascades and rivulets down a thousand feet to the sea. You are nothing in a little boat beneath those terrifying heights.

As the wind increased we worked for the shelter of Three Hummock Island that lay some miles further to windward. We still carried all sail but the jib, and the frequent squalls made necessary the most careful watchfulness in the handling of the boat.

We had passed the island on our last long southern tack; the next leg of our course would bring us in its lee. The sky to windward was dark with the murk of formless low-hanging clouds. The squalls were violent and laid us well on our beam. When we had come about on our last tack I relinquished the tiller and went below to prepare supper.

ADMIRALTY SOUND II

Then something happened. As if the whole accumulated forces of the wind had struck us, clattering and howling, we were beaten down. As I fell into a corner the whole place hurled itself upon me—table and stools and tins of food, the clock and the steaming supper. Somehow out of the hurtling confusion I laid hands upon the greatest mess of all, the sour dough, and held it upright—praise God, safe! For what seemed ages long the *Kathleen* lay that way, far over on her side; and then she slowly, slowly righted.

We lowered the mainsail in the howling squall, and double-reefed it; then we limped toward land. The deck had been washed clear of every unlashed thing.

"She's a good boat," said the mate, "or she'd never have come up."

"What do you do," I asked with affected ingenuousness a little later when we had made the shelter of the island, "when you're steering and a squall strikes you?"

"*You keep her off,*" answered the mate.

And as I now, a living man, sit here in the dry-land security of a Vermont hillside and record that answer of the mate, I *know* that there's a providence for fools.

I went ashore as soon as we had anchored, and the firm land seemed good again. I walked up the smooth pebble beach and entered the grove that bordered it. Here were canelo trees grown to a great size. Their bark is smooth like that of our beech and of a pinkish hue. The leaves are shaped like those of the laurel and are even a more polished brilliant green. Here among their branches flitted plump birds, like robins— but with light olive breasts and slate-green backs and brilliant orange legs and bills.

It was my custom at every port we made to go ashore with paints and canvas and make such a record of the place as the time at my disposal and the weather allowed. The wind and the sudden storms of rain often drove me to a makeshift shelter, where I would either wait out the storm or leave my gear to be reclaimed at another time. The day following our arrival at Three Hummock I walked to the northeastern end of the island carrying my paints and a large canvas. Across the sound towered the immense cathedral mountains of the north shore. It was a dull, moist day and against the dark precipices of the mountain face gleamed the silver of cascades that flowed from the melting snow and glaciers of the heights. I set up my canvas on the shore, bracing it against the wind with driftwood. But hardly had I begun to work when the rain came in torrents. I fled with my canvas to the shelter of a ledge of rock. Quickly I converted the picture into a roof, and, crawling under it, lay down huddled on the stones, while over me the rain beat on the canvas like the rolling of a kettle-drum. It was damp and cold; so, seeking refuge from discomfort, I fell asleep.

How long I slept I do not know. At last a silence awakened me. I crept out of my dark shelter into sunlight. The storm had passed and it was breathless calm. The wet rocks glistened and the shrubbery was hung with diamonds. But the mountains! Part sunlit and part veiled in trailing vapor shadows, illumined by the rainbow mist of swollen torrents, they stood for that one transient interlude peacefully and mildly beautiful.

During the three days that we remained at this island the wind either blew from the west or it was calm. It might have contented us there for as many weeks or months, for the island was of diverse character with many charming groves and wild meadows and a varied shore; and, lying as it did about midway in the sound, it commanded a view of the surrounding mountains that was not to be surpassed. But owing to the many delays that we had suffered, progress had now become an obsession to us and, if the Horn was to be reached, a necessity. So on the third day we fixed upon the next to sail—wind or no wind, fair wind or foul. And sail we did.

We turned out at four-fifteen to find the day already risen and the clouds of night dispersing toward the east to leave the heavens clear and blue. The wind, of course, was west. It had, moreover, blown most of the night and raised a choppy sea against us. We beat for hours, returning after every southward tack close to the shore of Three Hummock Island where, to our discouragement, we marked our slow advance. By ten o'clock, having progressed only as far as the mouth of Parry Harbor and knowing that we should not, by continuing, reach another port that day, we entered there. A dying wind bore us at length into Stanley Cove, where more than two weeks before we had anchored for one night.

(94)

NORTHWARD FROM THREE HUMMOCK ISLAND

It was quite different on this sunlit peaceful day; and two weeks had advanced the spring so that the lighter green of budding trees was mingled with the dark ever-greens, and young grass covered the bits of meadowland and fringed the beach. There on the shore beside a running brook we found again the framework of two Indian huts identical with those others that we had seen on Dawson Island. What-ever prompted the natives in the selection of their camp sites, it coincided with the judgment of our sense of quiet beauty. It may be that æsthetics are a sublimation of necessity.

The day continued mild and fair; and in the afternoon, a light breeze having risen, we set sail for Bahia Blanca, which is the southeast arm of Parry Harbor. We took the skiff in tow and, having in hand a couple of sheepskins that needed washing, tied them to a long line and towed them along, too.

Somewhere on the shore of Bahia Blanca was a small lumber mill; and our excur-sion there was prompted by a need of tobacco. We'll see the place, we thought, get the tobacco, and return to Stanley Cove tonight. And as we sailed serenely over that placid bay, with the sun shining on us and the whole region about us so quietly beautiful, we felt that a change of fortune had dawned on us, and that mild weather and prospering winds would henceforth attend our progress.

FROM STANLEY COVE

Meanwhile, unobserved by us, clouds had mounted in the west, till suddenly the sun was obscured; and with that shadow the glad mood of the day was gone. The mantle of clouds spread itself over the sky and it grew dark. The wind freshened. Gloriously we drove through the black water with crested waves racing at our side. Bahia Blanca opened up its length before us. Beyond its head was a lofty snow white region of mountains from which a broad glacier poured down to meet the bay.

"Look," cried one of us, "what is that smoke down on the water by the glacier?"

Clouds of smoke appeared driving across the water not only at the foot of the glacier but along the mountainous western shore. We were to learn, and that within a quarter of an hour, what fury of the wind that smoking sea betokened.

The wind had now become a gale, so that even with our mainsail reefed, as it was, we carried too much sail. The skiff at our stern was yawing and plunging frightfully, threatening at every moment to capsize, while the taut towline of our sheepskins made another hazard in the skiff's frantic career. We tried to pull the skiff alongside to draw it on board, but it had taken too much water to be manageable.

The confusion astern deterred us from coming up into the wind to take another reef, so, sailing as we were before the gale, we attempted to lower the mainsail. When the peak dropped, the sail filled like a balloon and the throat stuck fast. In an instant the mate was up the mast and trampling on it. Down with a run it came while the loose canvas beat wildly over everything. We hauled the plunging boom on board and secured it.

Meanwhile from behind a little wooded island some buildings had come into view on the western shore. We changed our course a few points to windward and held for them under the staysail; that was sail enough. There under the land we found the meaning of that smoking sea. The wind beat down upon us from the mountain side in furious squalls, lashing the water into spray and driving it over us in drenching clouds.

We near the land; and yet, beside the scant shelter of the island, no harbor reveals itself. But in the lee of that two boats lie tugging at their moorings. Riding high on a foaming sea, through streaming kelp and driving spray, we're there. There's a flopping of canvas and a long smooth glide into the wind, a rattle of the chain, a plunge, the vibrant rubbing of the hawser paying out; then suddenly it's calm and we ride at anchor. We look at each other then and laugh—and the whole galleried wilderness of forests toss their caps and roar.

While we furled the sails and set the deck in order, our eyes rested on the storm-swept bay. It had become a smoking maelstrom of fury.

CHAPTER XIV

TWO GENTLEMEN

WE lay barely fifty yards from the shore. Here, just above the tide's reach stood the long shed of the mill. Opposite this was a small building which, we came to know, was intended as the office and the house of the manager; and farther back, suggesting the third side of an open quadrangle that faced the bay, stood a long low building in which the men were quartered. Peering out at us from the sheltered cover of the mill shed stood a man. And though we greeted him with every wave of courtesy he made no answering sign, just watched us stolidly. It's no great pleasure to be stared at, stolidly; and we muttered our opinion of the ungracious fellow.

What was our delight, however, on rowing ashore, to have him meet us at the water's edge with the most winning smile of welcome, wading into the surf to seize our skiff and help us draw it up the beach!

"Bienvenida," said he, shaking our hands; and he bade us enter the house to get warm.

There, in the kitchen of the bunk house, with another man who presently appeared, we tasted of a hospitality that was to last for weeks and began a friendship that is not forgotten.

These two young Chilean lumberjacks, Don Antonio and "Curly" (it was all we ever learned to call him), revealed to us that gentlemen, in that romantic sense of "those who are possessed of good manners, kindness of heart, and strict integrity and honor," do flower in life beyond the reach of education and the traditions of culture. Little did these men know of the wide world; they were ignorant, illiterate, and superstitious. But even their Christian superstition had the grace of tolerance.

One dark night, Don Antonio related to me, when the wind was blowing every-

(98)

thing about the place, the devil came and set the machinery of the mill going and sawed some lumber. They found the new-sawn boards lying there in the morning.

"Did he do good work?" I asked.

"Lovely work," said Don Antonio. He was not a bigot.

Perhaps nothing moved me so much as their respect for my vocation and their unprompted recognition of its privacy. Only a painter can appreciate this high and grateful tribute that I pay them: they left me alone.

It cannot be said that we settled down at Bahia Blanca. We lived on board and lived in readiness for instant departure should the wind change to favor us; yet the establishment on shore became our headquarters by day, while between the Chileños, who were the sole occupants of the place, and ourselves there sprang up a pretty interchange of courtesies that never lacked a pleasant flavor of formality.

The one luxury of the mate's equipment on the *Kathleen* was a cheap, portable phonograph with a broken mainspring, and three cracked discs. The records were beyond repair; but I spliced and riveted the springs of the machine and, having but two sewing needles and no pins on board, made needles out of nails, and tempered them—and so the thing was made to emit an enjoyable, fragmentary, ghastly kind of music. We always carried the machine ashore, that and my silver flute.

I'd play the flute a while of an evening while everyone sat silent in polite attention. I would play the slow movements of Beethoven sonatas, "My Wandering Boy," and such like classical selections as my stiff fingers could accomplish. And at the conclusion they'd release their suppressed coughs and say "Lindo, muy lindo!"—which means "very lovely." And then on the phonograph, we'd have the undamaged last half of "Oh What a Pal Was Mary,"—and to that they would say "Lindo." So we were very happy. We'd eat heartily of roast mutton, have more music and a very little conversation, and with mutually repeated expressions of adieu be escorted to the shore.

The world has today become too small for some knowledge of the customs of all lands not to have penetrated even to the remotest wilderness. While our friends in Bahia Blanca knew nothing of our American political constitution, and little of our commercial and scientific achievements, they had been reached and impressed by North American art. Curly's hair was of a year's growth; he was a bit ashamed of it. It was indeed as immense a shock of curls, exuberant and black, as one might ever see. On learning that I was a barber he begged me to shear him. I had a perverse desire to crop those locks, but he deterred me.

"Give me," he said, "a real North American haircut." And he described it minutely.

Accordingly, adhering strictly to his instructions, I clipped the lower hair up to a sharp line about an inch above the ears, clipped it so close that the bleached scalp showed blue through the coarse stubble. Above that I left the black mass to flower

OUR ANCHORAGE—BAHIA BLANCA

like a huge chrysanthemum upon its stalk. With a professional flourish I removed the towel from my patron's neck, and presented him with the mirror.

"Lindo!" he cried, and "Lindo!" echoed Don Antonio coming in to view it. And smiling with all the happiness of pride, Curly thanked me, saying there was no one like a North American to cut hair. And that is what in Tierra del Fuego they know of America!

And so, between festivities and work, the days slid by. And the west wind either blew like fury or blew moderately, or there was no wind at all, and the mountains stood upon their heads reflected in the breathless calm of the green jade water of the bay. Sometimes our watchful eyes discovered that the clouds had changed their course. In wild excitement we would bid our friends good-bye, heave up anchor and sail out. But whatever currents might prevail among the clouds, down in that canyon of the sound there was no wind but west. We'd beat and drift and make a mile or two, and then, discouraged at such waste of time, turn tail and sheepishly come home.

At the head of Bahia Blanca is a wide glacial moraine that extends inland to the blue-green cliffs of the glacier. The broad glacial stream pours down from a remote inland region that appears as the very desolation of Antarctic winter. Flanking the glacier on the east is an immense flat mountain-dome of rock, covered with ice and spotless snow. Between this ice-capped dome and the nearer mountain of the north-east shore of Bahia Blanca is a broad valley bearing southeasterly. No barrier of mountains appears beyond the relatively low horizon of this valley, so that it seems to be a highway leading south.

It was from the top of a little hill that stood at the edge of the moraine that I first saw this view; and then, and the many other times that I sat upon that sheltered hillside facing it, I was possessed by its beauty and moved to ponder on the insistent yet illusive significance that it contained for me.

Is it mere chance that the forms and humors of nature appear as symbols of the moods, experiences and desires of the human spirit? The unbroken pathways of the wilderness are reminders of the hard and solitary way that ardent souls must travel. The glittering, virgin whiteness of high mountain-fields of snow, untrodden, maybe unattainable, their mist-veiled beauty neither earth nor cloud, remote, serene and passionless, picture the spirit's aspiration. Can it have been the fervid imagination of man that has endowed these mountains with an aura of symbolism? Rather is it the reality of mountains and plains, the sea and the unfathomable heavens, unchangingly forever dominating man, cradling him in that remote hour of his awakening into consciousness, forever smiling, brooding, thundering upon him, that have imposed their nature upon man and made him what he is.

And still, even where men dwell in the environment of their own creation, the wilderness casts its light and shadow into their dreams. Trees murmur in the city's night; men hear the thunder and the wash of seas. The moon's light shines to them on silver peaks; the wild, eternal glory of the universe appears. Unrest possesses them, and they awake to the adventurous courage of their race's past, and go.

It is not choice that draws men from comfort and security into the hazards of adventure or the miseries of solitude, but rather an impulse profounder than consciousness and more forceful than reason. It may be likened to a reassertion of the will to the achievement of high purpose. And in that the denials and perils that are sought resemble the soul-paths of virtue is concealed the truth that nature is the parent of our moral thought.

There as I sat one afternoon upon that sheltered hillside and viewed the varied beauty of the scene veiled in mistlike rain, the plain traversed by intersecting glacial streams of milky water and islanded with groves of trees and bits of meadowland, the lower mountains clothed in forests of the deepest green, the high slopes red with budding shrubbery, the dazzling summits, and the valley that forever seemed a highway to a promised land—then, as I looked far up that valley's green-clad, gently rising plain to where it dipped from view and left the whole beyond a mystery, a strange thing came to pass. The grey mist of the rain became transfused with golden light and in the broad gap where my eyes were fixed gleamed a pale rainbow. It was only for a moment; then the mists dispersed and sunlight flooded everything. That was November the twenty-fourth.

Under that date my diary reads: "It is at last dark after the long twilight, and the lights of the men's house and on the *Kathleen* are extinguished. I sit in the bare, wood-walled room of one of the mill outbuildings at a window overlooking the water. Rain beats upon the panes. Squalls sweep the bay and the surf roars on the shore. The breeze that penetrates around the window sash flutters my candle. The wind blows straight in upon us from the northwest; it never changes. We have given up all hope of sailing west and southward, for we could never beat out through this sound and Gabriel Channel. It is a conclusion that we have found hard to face.

"However, we will continue southward—on foot; and on the day after tomorrow we will start up the valley from the head of Bahia Blanca."

There is always a fascination in assembling the equipment and provisions for an expedition, whether it be for a picnic luncheon in the country or for a cruise of many months. This time the certain difficulties of the enterprise that we were undertaking and the uncertainty of the time that it would occupy us imposed the attractively conflicting problem of loads both light and comprehensive. Moreover, the problem of supplies was complicated by our penury. We were heading to be sure, for the town of Ushuaia, where undoubtedly meals could be obtained and supplies purchased. But for this we had no money. And while there was the possibility of someone's befriending us with a few days' board, we had no thought of obtaining credit. Yet somehow Cape Horn was to be reached, and to that time if not beyond it we must live.

But even more of an encumbrance than our food supplies were the heavy materials of my unfortunate profession; and allied to these were the cameras. The kodak would have been enough, but I had not entirely succeeded in repairing the damaged shutter and it was good for only very short exposures. So the bulky Graflex had to go. And there was the flute. I don't know definitely why I carried it about, for sometimes for days I would not play upon it; but then would come an hour when above all other useful things the flute alone was a necessity.

So after the most studied consideration I began assembling the equipment. As things were passed on deck and checked off on my list the mate loaded them into the skiff and carried them ashore to a room that had been put at our disposal in the manager's house. And when this had been accomplished I went ashore with my list and checked them over. And it was then that a most lamentable thing occurred, the very memory of which fills me with shame.

"Where," I asked the mate after I had thoroughly inspected the equipment, "is the revolver?"

"I put it on the table," he replied.

Together we went through everything; it was clearly not there. Although both the mate and I recalled its having been brought ashore I went aboard again and searched. We searched the path from the shore, and the skiff—in vain.

And always the mate affirmed that he had put it on the table.

(102)

WIND-TORN TREES

No room for doubt was left; and with an ugly conviction I went to Don Antonio and told him what had occurred.

It was not till he had himself searched carefully through our effects that he would credit what I had told him. "He is a very honest man," he said of Curly; and much perplexed, he went to speak to him.

As I saw it afterwards, Curly's quiet, hurt denial of the charge was more expressive of his innocence, of his entire innocence of any comprehension of theft, than anger would have been. And it made my subsequent remorse more poignant.

That denial ended it as far as I concerned myself; the gun was gone.

It was an hour later when the receding tide exposed the revolver to the searching eyes of Don Antonio.

Our equipment now lay ready to be made into the two packs. It was as follows:

Salt	Tooth Powder	Revolver
Sugar	Nails	Ammunition
Eggs	Cameras	Blankets
Milk	Films	Razors
Dried Soup	Paper	Brush
Tea	Paints	Socks

Baking Powder	Tobacco	Shoes
Flour	Pipes	Needle and Thread
Chocolate	Candles	Flute
Corn Meal	Lantern	Tent
Frying Pan	Bandage	Barometer
Cups	Credentials	Ground Cloth
Spoons	Painting Materials	Compass
Kettles	Brushes	Lasso
Bacon	Medium	Wire
Pail	Paints	Tacks
Soap	Canvas	Whetstone
Tooth Brush	Stretchers	Axe

CHAPTER XV

THE RAINBOW PATH

BEFORE dawn of that momentous day, November twenty-fourth, we were up and dressed. Energy again possessed us, for the decision to abandon the boat had broken the inertia that had become the habit of our days, and set us free again for action. While the mate cooked breakfast I went ashore and roused our two friends; half an hour later, having made everything secure on board, we left the *Kathleen;* I was never, as it proved, to tread her deck again.

The equipment for our expedition had been made into two packs, each weighing sixty pounds. Loading these into the small boats belonging to the mill, we embarked in company with the two Chileños, who had proposed to be our guides over the few miles of our route with which they were familiar, and proceeded to row diagonally across the bay toward a cove at the head on the northeastern side. The day was overcast; and any last misgivings that we felt as to the wisdom of the step that we were taking were mercifully disposed of—for the wind again was west.

It was low tide and our landing was made on a slippery rocky shore along which, moreover, we had to struggle for a quarter of a mile at the great hazard, laden as we were, of breaking our legs and necks at the very outset of our journey.

On reaching the head of the cove we struck inland across the marshland and bog that composed the border of the moraine. And if anything could have deterred us from continuing it must have been those first fatiguing miles. We presently, however, reached dry soil again and in the cool depths of a vaulted forest laid our packs aside and rested. It was quiet in that sheltered sanctuary. The long dark aisles were here and there illuminated by shafts of sunlight that filtered through the tracery of leaves as through rose-windows of stained glass; and everywhere the rich green velvet of

LAST GLIMPSE OF PARRY HARBOR

the forest floor was starred with yellow violets. That forest was in truth a church of vast and solemn sanctity. The stillness was its music: the solitude its invocation. And the more as our devotion was unconscious did it purge our souls of their vague tremors: for here the wilderness disclosed its peacefulness.

We had heard and read too much of the virtual impenetrability of the mountain regions of Tierra del Fuego and in our short inland excursions had experienced enough of the difficulties of travelling there not to have realized that in attempting to cross the virgin wilderness of Brecknock Peninsula our endurance might be taxed to its very limit. While there are two established routes across the mountains from the north to Beagle Channel, these are at the eastern end of Lago Fognano where the mountain ranges are less lofty and rugged. The farthest western passage was made by the explorer priest Padre Agostini when, accompanied by an Italian Alpine mountaineer, he crossed with great hazard and difficulty from near the outlet of Lago Fognano. Considering Brecknock Peninsula as extending westward from the head of Admiralty Sound, there is no record of its having been crossed: and certainly the lofty Valdivieso and Darwin range present a barrier that might well deter men from attempting it. Nevertheless, a serviceable passage across the peninsula would considerably shorten the route from Punta Arenas to Ushuaia.

(107)

To the two Chileños, accustomed as they were to the imprisonment of the wilderness, this seemed a mad adventure that we were embarking on. We, however, looked only at its accomplishment and felt the exhilaration and confidence of men released by their own decision to follow on a quest that difficulties had but exalted to a passion. And if at first our untrained bodies staggered under their unaccustomed loads our hearts were light and we were careless of fatigue and of what unknown trials might confront us.

After a few minutes' rest in the forest we reshouldered our packs and continued on our way. We presently emerged into open country to ascend a mounting succession of hillocks, on reaching whose last summit we paused again and rested, with the view to justify us. Behind us lay the bay that we had left and the far mountains of the sound, and before us—almost at our feet, so near they seemed in their immensity— the turquoise cliffs of the glacier. The sloping ice field of its surface vanished upwards in a bank of clouds that hid the mountains of its source: so that its own rim seemed to touch the sky as if beyond it there were nothing.

A guanaco, browsing across the plain, took fright at us and dashed away. Over our heads a condor soared with motionless wings, slowly, in great circles, passing and repassing so close that we could count the outspread feathers of his wing tips. And, as he turned, the sun gleamed on his sleek, black sides.

Then down we plunged to the level of the plain again, crossed a deep stream and, following it, entered the forest of the valley. But here where the way might have been difficult were smooth guanaco paths, so that we travelled on them almost at a trot. Up hill and down we went, for the river now flowed through a gorge that was impossible to follow closely. Yet always we approached that wooded summit that from the bay had been the farthest we could see. Then came a hard, steep climb—and we were there.

We saw below us a broad, flat, grassy plain with the winding river flowing through it. The mountains rose abruptly on the north and south, but at the far end, over a barrier of lower hills, opened the gap of our valley, still leading on. Descending to the plain, we made our way across the marshy ground to meet the stream: and there, overshadowed by a cliff perhaps a thousand feet in height, we stopped for lunch.

With consideration that was characteristic of them our two friends partook but sparingly of the simple meal of bread and tea that we spread for them, insisting that we conserve our provisions lest we have need of them on our journey. This last thoughtfulness of those kind fellows lingers in my mind, for it was here that we left them. They embraced us affectionately, wished us good fortune and a quick return, and we parted on our opposite ways.

On reaching the end of the plain we began the ascent of a succession of steep hills, whose tangled slopes, the guanaco paths having eluded us, offered the most trying obstacles to progress. We struggled through thickets of dwarfed trees choked with

NOON OF THE FIRST DAY

thorny underbrush and fallen trunks, across a small stream, and up sheer banks and hillsides. And every hill we climbed, while it appeared to be the last, proved but the threshold of another.

At thirteen hundred feet we reached the top. It was above the timber line and from its bare summit we looked down over the wide plain that we had passed and over the wooded ridge from which we had descended to it, to the far-away blue mountains of Bahia Blanca. Here where we stood the mountains crowded close and pinched the valley, and the overflowing ice-cap of the northern range hung as if suspended over us, immense and terrifying. Yet, but a little way below us and beyond, was a most peaceful little flat of meadowland, with a winding stream and a pond with wild geese swimming on it; and near at hand at the river's source was a small glacier, gleaming like a jewel against the somber earth-tones of the rocks and shrubbery. Spring had already entered here, and the winter's snow that must have deeply covered everything had vanished but for the drifts remaining in the sheltered clefts.

Down on that plain against the sheltering hillside we threw off our burdens and rested. And, I may record, the echoes of that peaceful place were for the first time— and, we may believe, the last, forever—awakened to expression by the sweet and plaintive tones of the silver flute. Yet that was a delusion, for man at last was come; and my revolver shot that killed a goose told more truly of his coming.

(109)

Two condors soared about, not far above us as we sat there resting; and presently there appeared a guanaco. He ascended a spur of the mountain and was lost to sight.

Beyond the meadow we again ascended a small succession of stony hills and at fourteen hundred feet stood upon the watershed of the defile. And now at last the long valley lay before us and justified our faith in the road that we had chosen. Between straight mountain walls it lay for twenty miles, an undulating downward-sloping plain varied with groves and meadows, hills and streams, that in the aura of the far away appeared a cultivated scene. The foreground was a rock-strewn plain not difficult to travel on.

Over the plain on every hand grazed guanacos; we counted nearly a hundred of them. Some showed great curiosity at our presence and bounded toward us. On near approach they grew more cautious, pausing, advancing again timidly, retreating in sudden panic to return again to look at us. One, bolder than the rest, after each flight came closer. Then at last with great assurance he approached deliberately. Reaching a knoll not fifty yards away, he stood there motionless, regarding us. We remained stock-still lest our movements should again alarm him. At last, his curiosity satisfied, he lay down. Nor was he disturbed when we again walked on; and it was only to pass near to us at a mad run that he left his place of observation. Down the hill he bounded over the boulder-strewn plain. Reaching the stream he leaped it with finished grace and finally, with pace unslackened, disappeared among the trees.

As we advanced the difficulties increased. Our course on the right bank of the stream became impeded here and there by bog and dwarfed trees or by ravines and precipitous hillsides. As always, then, the other shore looked better. But the stream had accumulated such volume that to cross it without a thorough wetting became a problem. At last, at a narrow place where the rapids raced between steep walls of rock, we managed it. Of course, it was no better there.

We reached a forest where the stream flowed in many channels over a broad gravel bed: there on the river bank in the darkness of twilight and the falling rain we made our camp.

It was but a few minutes' work to pitch the little sleeping tent; and while the mate plucked the goose I built a fire and hung the kettle over it to boil. And presently with the goose well roasted on a spit, we sat there feasting in the utmost comfort, by the fire's warmth made heedless of the rain.

I think I was too tired to sleep: the ground was hard and the cold dampness seemed to penetrate the blankets. And my sleeping mate's proximity forced me to rigidly forego such exercise as might have restored the circulation of my limbs. It was a welcome dawn that came at last.

At seven we were on our way. From the very beginning we found hard going. The way was steep and obstructed with tangled underbrush. Occasional tributary streams to the main river crossed our path; and while none of them was of sufficient depth to

LAND LEGS

GLACIER NEAR THE VALLEY'S SUMMIT

have hindered our wading it, we would not readily submit to the discomfort of wet clothes. The valley proved at close hand to be more broken into minor hills and dales than our first distant view of it had discovered, and the meadowlands, alas, proved bog. It was after we had been for an hour or more immersed in the entanglements of the jungle that we again attained a height from which we held an unobstructed view of the valley. The day was grey but clearer than the day before, and beyond the varied slope in the blue haze of the distance appeared a vast plain enclosed, apparently, by mountains. Yet that it somehow opened toward the sea the streams were evidence.

At last the main river again impeded our path; and rather than follow it to where against the northern range it flowed through a deep gorge, we undertook to cross it. The river here was deep and swift and for an hour we were occupied in bridging it with a long tree trunk. With this accomplished we carried our packs across and continued dry-shod.

It often seemed that whatever way, after careful deliberation, we chose was the wrong one; the left bank, if we trod the right, soon smiled at us invitingly; and if we forsook the river entirely for the illusion of another route, new obstacles appeared to reproach us for our bad judgment. So it was not long after our triumphant, dry-

ONE CROSSING PLACE

shod crossing of the river before we encountered a barrier of precipitous land whose ascent was more exhausting than five miles of average travelling. It is not the distance that one covers laden with a pack that tires one but the occasional obstacles. Legs soon become accustomed to the load and do the work of normal walking uncomplainingly. But let the way become obstructed and one becomes soon conscious of fatigue. And when toward the day's end the laden, tired traveller is confronted by a fallen tree, too high to clamber over and too near the ground to admit his crawling under it encumbered with the pack—then speaks the broken spirit with the wish that here might be the journey's end.

But in the main the travelling was not difficult and but for an accident to the mate we should have been in the highest spirits. We had reached good ground and were tramping briskly down the valley when he first spoke of a pain in his right foot, and admitted that he had endured it for some hours. An examination revealed no bruise and we attributed it vaguely to a strain. Nevertheless, throughout our journey it gave constant and increasing trouble, landing him eventually in a week's confinement to his bed.

(114)

The afternoon was well advanced, when, emerging from a forest of tall trees that clothed an elevation, we came again upon the river, sheer below us, a wide stream flowing over gravel flats. There we stopped and lit a fire, and rested—for we were tired, and had a lunch of bread and tea—for we were very hungry.

We had no choice but to cross the river again and no choice but to wade it. Removing shoes and stockings we accomplished this, although the glacier water was as cold as ice, and to our infinite joy found on the other side a smooth guanaco path. For miles we followed it along the stream through meadowland and woods; and at last where the shore was marshy it led us to the dry mountain side, yet still continued on our way. There, in the primeval forest was again the grandeur and the hallowed stillness that had been our benediction in the forest of Bahia Blanca, and there again were yellow violets starring the green carpet of the floor.

As we sat and rested by a fallen giant tree that blocked the path we heard guanacos calling below us in the near-by thicket of the plain. Theirs is a strange cry, a prolonged whinny yet with the timbre of a palpitating quack. I answered it and to my great joy found that my reply attracted them. From several spots arose their clamorous calls. Nearer and ever nearer they came while still I answered. Finally we heard the crackling of branches, and two guanacos emerged from the thicket but a little way from us. What they expected to find I don't know: certainly not men. Discovering us they stopped short in their tracks; they looked at us for a moment and then, in panic, fled.

Here it came to me that I had left my cap at our last resting place, and I returned to find it. While I was reproaching myself for thus wasting my strength and our time, I was rewarded by the discovery of the decaying frames of two Indian shelters. I was to learn in Ushuaia that in former years, when the English mission at that place was active, there had appeared occasional bands of Indians of the Alacaloof race, who by some unknown and difficult way had come across the mountains from the north. It was undoubtedly their traces that we'd hit upon.

We walked until nightfall; and then, where the dry forest land again reached to the river bank, we pitched our camp. Wild fowl were everywhere in abundance, but we contented ourselves with the fried remains of our goose. We were very happy—all had gone so well; and a special contentment is for those who are so fortunate as to bear their goods and house upon their backs, for where they stop—no matter in what wilderness—is home.

Seven of the morning saw us again upon our way: and this day from the outset we encountered such continuous hard going that the rare smooth stretches stand in my memory as garden spots. After some hours of clambering along the steep slope of the mountain side, where fallen trees and thickets everywhere obstructed us, we came upon a plain of short-cropped pasture land: our relief at treading that firm and unobstructed ground was as if the burdens had fallen from our shoulders. Then, too, the day was fair, and for the first time we saw the valley with the cheerful sunlight over it. We were on the border of that plain that on the morning of the day before had been visible to us in the blue haze of the distance. It was flat as the surface of a sea and islanded with groves; and the west wind swept the grass to waves of golden sheen. But the firm land was of short extent and on the course that we had laid straight down the center of the valley we soon encountered marshy soil that it was misery to travel over. Yet to the eye it was ever so alluring; and, in the belief that it must change for better, we held on. The marshland became bog, and that deceptive bog was velvet smooth with moss and not a mound or bush was there to mar its far extent. Its beauty was more eloquent than past experience, and we struck out into it.

The first quarter of a mile was soft and we sank above our shoe tops, and the cold water oozed around our toes; the second quarter of a mile was softer so that we sank halfway to our knees and had to tread nimbly at that; the third quarter—we still held on like fools, hoping for firmer soil—found us wallowing. We were tired. We removed our packs and rested on them. And then, almost in a panic at this treacherous thing that threatened to engulf us, we turned and struggled back to safety.

There was nothing to do but seek the firm soil of the mountain side again. But unfortunately our path had followed a sort of peninsula of the prairie, and to reach the nearer northern mountains we had either to retrace our steps for several miles or cross a marsh that intervened between the prairie meadow and the mountain side. We chose the marsh. When one gets thoroughly wet he doesn't care. We leaped upon the huge tussocks that stood like beehives out of the water. Sometimes we landed fairly upon them and kept our balance, sometimes we slipped off again and plunged into the water; and at last, there remaining little about us to be kept dry, we waded through regardless of the wet. Reaching the mountain side at last, we threw our packs aside, built a great fire, removed our soaking clothes and hung them up to dry, stretched ourselves out in the fire's warmth, and rested.

The mate's foot was giving him great pain. It appeared to be the arch that had been strained. I whittled a splint for it and bound it up with sticking plaster: this afforded temporary relief. We were unfortunately not well supplied with shoes. The mate had a pair of well worn, high, moccasin-type boots which I had given him, and a pair of flimsy pointed oxfords. I had but one pair that could be worn: they were comfortable, square-toed working boots; they were old—having been thrice re-soled —but were still serviceable; but being low they were always filled with water. I carried another pair of boots that were a delight to the eye and a misery to the feet; strong, high moccasins, the very thing for such an expedition, they had developed the least little wrinkle, from whose steady, gentle and excruciating pressure on the tendon of the heel no device of splint or bandage could relieve me. I plead not ignorance but poverty that we were travelling so ill supplied.

But that day held surprises for us of the most startling nature. It must be remem-

RAINBOW VALLEY

bered that we journeyed through an unknown region toward the remote destination of Ushuaia, which, so far as we knew, was the most westerly inhabited spot on the south shore of Tierra del Fuego. Of the rate of our progress we had no means of judging. We had walked approximately twelve hours a day, but our route was tortuous and beset with obstacles that impeded and delayed us. More than that our track had been southeasterly we knew nothing. It was perhaps two hours after we had extricated ourselves from the bog before we again yielded to the allurements of the plain to leave the tree-strewn mountain side.

This time it was a dry woodland flat that tempted us. Travelling rapidly along smooth paths we soon came to a rushing torrent whose channel was heaped with refuse of the forest. We built a bridge and crossed it and were about to enter the forest on the other side when suddenly—like Crusoe discovering the savage's footprints in the sand—we saw on the smooth brown forest turf the prints of horses' feet. We stared at them in bewildered joy; yet hardly had a surmise of their significance entered our heads when we were startled by a trampling of horses.

There were four of them. How and whence they came concerned us later: our first thought was to capture one or more of them. But though we practiced every lure with salt and meal and stealthily crept near them with the lasso, they were entirely mistrustful, and soon galloped away into the forest.

But there remained with us the knowledge that we had reached the frontier of a settlement, and the elation of having somehow neared our journey's end. Yet we had many weary miles to go and the discouragement to face that day of being separated by deep streams and impassable bog from the dry hillside where we came to know our destination lay.

It was late that afternoon and we still toiled along the cluttered mountain slopes; below us flowed a deep stream with the sodden plain of marsh and bog beyond it; it was hot, and mosquitoes swarmed about us, adding their pestering stings as a last torture to our weariness; across the valley shone the low sun upon green pastures over whose slopes crept tiny spots of white: for an hour—long before they came to view—we had heard, faintly from far away, the lowing of cattle and the bleat of sheep. Yet we couldn't cross.

And at nightfall, disheartened by the very nearness of the unattainable and too tired to be cheered by that we'd brought our journey's end within our reach, we camped in a depression of the steep mountain side. Sitting in the smoke of the camp fire we devoured our supper. We crawled into the little tent, drew the mosquito netting behind us, and slept.

CHAPTER XVI

THE FOURTH DAY

WITH dawn we leapt to action. Gone was the whole weariness of the night before. There, less than a mile away—for the valley narrowed at this point—were the pasture hillsides that we meant to reach; and the mere streams and bog that had deterred us now were nothing. We felled a tree that almost reached across the stream, and with dead limbs we bridged the rest of it. We crossed dry-shod, and, recking nothing, plunged into the bog. We followed different tracks and it became a joke between us who should sink the deeper. We wallowed, sinking deep at times and struggling out again. One moment I went in above my thighs: I threw my pack off and crawled out upon it. And we got across.

Now the river confronted us. It was wide and deep. There was no way to bridge it —and we didn't care. We were too wet—and eager. Choosing the broadest spot to cross it we strode in. It rose to our knees, to our thighs, to our waists—a little higher and the swift current would have swept us off our feet: and then it dropped. Thighs, knees appeared again; ankle deep we raced out through the gravelly shoals and gained dry land.

In a little sheltered pasture clearing where the bars of a man-made fence were in the view to gladden us, we lit a fire, doffed our clothes, and hung them up to dry.

There being no habitation in sight, it was our plan to continue down the valley in the knowledge that eventually it must lead us to the sea: there, or somewhere on the way, we counted upon finding the establishment to which these pasture lands belonged. While in this conjecture we were partly wrong, such a course would, nevertheless, have brought us more quickly to Ushuaia than that which circumstances

(119)

determined we should pursue. We had resumed our packs and were striding merrily along in beaten cattle paths upon our chosen way. Northward across from us stood the wooded range along whose base we had toiled. Occasional peaks lifted their high summits into the region of winter—but all the rest was verdant with late spring. Our eyes were following the curving river's course along the valley as it appeared, was lost, and reappeared among the groves of trees that grew in scattered clumps along the shore, when suddenly emerged a moving form, a horseman galloping on the river bank.

At my sudden shout he stopped and looked about as if amazed: and then he saw us on the pasture hillside. He turned his horse and rode a devious way to meet us. At last he reappeared and with astonishment upon his face rode up and greeted us. And when we told him whence we had come, there came into his face a wonder as if we had been angels dropped from heaven. We were, he told us, at an outlying camp of the Estancia Austral of Yendegaia Bay, on Beagle Channel, and but a little distance from the head of Lapataia Bay. He told us that we were certainly the first ever to have crossed there from the north.* The realization that we were discoverers filled us with immense elation.

He was a good-hearted, generous fellow, this Chileño shepherd, by name Francisco; a great, powerful, sloppy, dirty, easy-going, easy-natured chap. His house was like a dog kennel, a miserable shanty of two little rooms—a filthy, dirt-floored kitchen, if one had a mind to call it that, and an untidy bunk room—but he made it ours with the gesture of one who gave us all he had. In his enthusiasm over our exploit he demanded that we recount it over and over again. A short, cheap road to Punta Arenas it meant to him, a way of escape from employers whose petty meanness, we were to learn, made their service a degradation.

Francisco prevailed upon us to ride with him to the estancia, and the following morning was set for the trip. He appeared to contemplate a kind of showman's pride in thus displaying us, and he dwelt upon the enthusiasm with which our discovery of the pass would be received by his patrones. Meanwhile, the day was before us; and after a lunch of hot milk and sour bread we mounted two horses, a mare and a gelding, and rode off upon an excursion toward Lapataia Bay.

We had just passed out of the enclosed pasture into the open range when we were set upon by two stallions; and throughout the two hours of our ride this jealous, lustful pair furnished no end of diversion and excitement; and finally upon a naked hilltop, rearing aloft in locked embrace above the mountain peaks, they staged with thundering hoof-beats and the screams of bitten rage and pain a conflict of such

*It is mentioned in an old missionary report from Ushuaia that bands of Alacaloofs, the Indians of the northern channels, appeared occasionally at the mission, having crossed from Admiralty Sound. They reported great difficulties on the way, deep streams, mountains and valleys. These Indians, being unused to land travel, may have exaggerated the difficulties. The remains of Indian shelters that we found would indicate our route as being the one travelled by the Alacaloofs. Our subsequent inquiries confirmed that we were the first white discoverers of the pass.

VIRGIN FOREST

WILD PASTURE LAND, RAINBOW VALLEY

frenzied violence and power as for magnificence of beauty one may never see surpassed.

On the return to camp we found another guest there, one of a gang of road builders at work in the forest some miles away; and we found a banquet of mutton stew. We were in clover; and the tranquil, cloudless, golden evening was as a mirror of our contentment, and a prophecy, we might have thought, of the morrow's fair-weather welcome to Estancia Austral.

To begin with, while there were plenty of horses there was but one saddle, and this Francisco—naturally enough—took for himself. He appeared magnificently accoutered with a poncho to his knees and my tall painful boots, which I had given him, adorning his legs. A horse was provided for our packs and two for us; and in lieu of saddles we had a sheepskin each. And so at about ten in the morning we set out. We rode for hours over a good track through pasture land and forest and broad meadows. It appeared to be Francisco's pleasant humor at times to test our horsemanship, and where occasion offered he'd spur his horse into a mad gallop and lead the way over ditches and brooks, looking back the while with a devilish grin on his face. The mate's unfamiliarity with the gait of a horse was more than recompensed by the strength of his legs. Gripping his steed with those giant forceps he became as one

FROM FRANCISCO'S CAMP

with it; and if the spectacle he furnished—leaning forward, elbows out, and flying coat-tails—was curious, only a formalist would criticize his horsemanship.

Arrived at a gate some two miles from our destination, our guide told us to dismount. Removing the bridles and sheepskins from our horses, he concealed them in the underbrush. Then, while he kept the two unsaddled horses from the gate, we slipped through and closed it. He gave me his horse to ride and walked alongside.

"That's so the patrón won't know we've used the horses," he said with a grim laugh. But it was only when we met the patrón that we comprehended the wisdom of his caution.

About us now were the developments of a prospering enterprise—cleared land, fences, constructed roads and substantial bridges. An extensive flat is at the head of Yendegaia Bay and in the midst of this stood the barns and sheds. Two men were there at work.

"The old patrón," said Francisco, recognizing one of them from a distance.

CHAPTER XVII

THE MAD ONE

THE two men—"two devils, old and crabbed," reads my diary—looked up at our approach. One of them, beyond his comic long, red, swollen nose, is not remembered; the other, the patrón, was a tall powerful man of maybe sixty. He was rather a handsome fellow, but with an unwholesome yellow complexion, a hard, shrewd smile, and eyes that advertised his cunning. It was his nature to keep his own counsel, trust no one, and give nothing. Bezmalinovich, for that was his name, was a type of the Croat or Dalmatian race as they appear in South America. By that rascality which, operating through hard dealings, is called ability, and by miserly thrift in the hoarding of mean earnings, he had become in a small way a capitalist; and he was now the chief proprietor of the establishment whose hospitality through ill advice we sought.

I don't know what this fellow thought of us: whether he took us to be escaped convicts from Ushuaia, free-lancing desperadoes or mere vagabonds, a cynical smile played about his lips while we recounted the manner of our coming; and before we had concluded he shrugged his shoulders and walked off.

There was nothing to do but approach him again. We told him that we had come there at the request of his shepherd, who believed that our information would be of interest to him, and that we were now upon our way to Ushuaia. At that he laughed.

"Why, you can't walk there!" he said. "It's eight hours by horseback; and, besides, you can't cross the river on foot."

At our suggestion that he lend us horses he shrugged his shoulders, said there were but three horses on the farm and that anyhow he had nothing to do with it. "Ask the patrón," he said.

Don Antonio, the young patrón, to whom the elder had referred us, soon appeared. He was a mild young fellow with a flabby hand, a very decent kindly man at heart, but so pathetically under the dominance of the old devil that he couldn't call his soul his own. He only repeated what the other had said about the horses—adding, however, that we might go to the house and get some bread.

Francisco drew a sullen face when we rejoined him with our tale, and in disgusted silence we rode on down to the house.

It is possible that if our reception had been slightly less unfriendly we would not have stayed; certainly if it had been more so, or if we had not been fortified by the sympathetic fellow feeling of the Chilean subjects of this Croat kingdom, we *could* not have remained. Their gratuitous discourtesy had, however, passed into the ludicrous; and if subsequent affronts were disconcerting, our humor saved us from feeling humiliated. We accepted them and sat tight; and that buffoonery of rudeness became the object of our amused reflections upon the Croat character.

Beside the two old men and Don Antonio there were of that race the cook and two young foremen. These, with the exception of the cook, constituted, in opposition to the Chileños, of whom there were four, an aristocracy that was better quartered and better fed and to whom as a body the social privilege of the warm kitchen was open.

We stayed. When mealtime came no one prevented our taking a place on the benches at the men's table and helping ourselves to mutton and bread. When bedtime came we went unhindered into the bunk room and made our beds upon the floor. Several times, as if by arrangement together, the Croat lords came and requested us to recount the details of our journey; they invariably looked at each other and shrewdly smiled—and believed nothing. They addressed neither a good-morning to us nor a good-night—except that once Don Antonio, on returning unexpectedly to the house, found himself alone with us and entered with such friendliness into conversation that it appeared as an apology.

By far the most interesting character in the place was the cook. Juan Rompuela (as well as I can decipher his cramped and shaky autograph as it appears in my diary under the portrait I drew of him) was a man of sixty-five. I remember him chiefly by a few acts of the most sensitive kindness—and yet these, being contradicted by less tangible expressions of Croat meanness, suggested the torment that must have caused his malady: the cook was mad. I had caught but occasional glimpses of this strange person until, the supper dishes having been cleared away and the kitchen put in order, he came and joined the men who sat in conversation around the table. My pack, from which I had removed a few articles, lay in one corner of the room and the men, noticing my flute, had asked me to play. It must be the first rule of such vagabondage as we practiced to accede to every request for entertainment; and, with all the embarrassment of a performing schoolboy, I got out the instrument, moistened my wind-parched lips, and launched upon my limited repertory.

(125)

USHUAIA

I cannot say—touching as the telling of it would appear—that at my plaintive notes these rough men's souls were moved to tears; I can't say truly that they were moved at all. After the first flash of novelty was over they resumed their conversation, but considerately, in subdued tones. The cook, however, having seated himself close to me, leaned forward, and with his eyes fixed upon me as if enthralled with wonder, listened with a profound and moved attention that communicated itself to me. His was a strange emaciated visage, wrinkled in a manner that betrayed rather the torturings of emotion than what is deemed character. The line was straight from the projecting forehead to the point of the long chin, and his red, opera-bouffe nose projected straight out like a thing stuck on. His long, unkempt hair gave him the appearance of a wild man; but it was the look, the stare of impotent intensity of his little bulging eyes, that told his madness.

At the first sound of the flute the old patrón appeared. It was his habit when the humor was upon him to join the men in gossip or at cards; and invariably at his appearance the jovial spirit of the gathering changed to one of constraint. And when with a clap upon some fellow's back and a sardonic laugh he cracked a joke, it was received as dolefully as a hangman's pun. Hearing the flute, he had entered. He stood for a moment staring at me with his invariable smile of inner malice; then, seating himself at the table opposite to me he began with deliberate offence to sing another tune.

"Don't mind him," muttered the mad cook in German, drawing closer, "he is ignorant and doesn't appreciate music."

Presently the patrón retired and wine and cards appeared. It was nearly dark but the long twilight lingered on; and through the glassed enclosure of the sun porch where the gathering sat appeared the cold, stark panorama of the bay and mountains, an inarticulate immensity of which the heated riot of the card game seemed the heart. But my reflections upon the symbolism of the mountain and the candle, of the sea and the passion of the human spirit, upon what things are done "where men and mountains meet" were disturbed by the turn of cook-baiting that the entertainment took, and quite shattered by discovering that after all the picturesque Spanish playing cards were made in Cleveland, Ohio.

The game broke up with the poor cook screaming with frenzy at some real or fancied swindling he had been the victim of. At last, still muttering his rage, he left the crowd to its laughter and went to bed. The rest of us soon followed.

On entering the bunk room I found the cook just turning back the coverlet of his bed, which he had made up neatly and which, unlike the other bunks, was furnished with a pillow slip and sheets.

"This is for you, señor," he said.

"But where are you going to sleep?" I asked him.

"Oh—anywhere," he answered, indicating the floor.

(127)

With the bunks all occupied, there was certainly nowhere else; so against the old man's persistent entreaties I declined his sacrifice.

It was a stinking place, that bunk room, with seven dirty men packed in it and the door and window shut; but I was tired, and soon the fetid, rumbling darkness of the squalid room passed from my consciousness.

What was it! Out of a warmth and comfort that was oblivion to the body my mind emerged into a dreaming consciousness of dainty, tinkling music; and the untrammeled imagination wove out of these fairy strands of sound a world of timeless, incorporeal loveliness. Slowly that dream awakened me as I evoked the power of my mind to grasp and make more real the tracery of that sweet illusion. And presently, still lying there with eyes tight shut hearing that fairy tune in tinkling repetition, I recognized it as a German melody:

MEIN HUT DER HAT DREI ECK-EN, DREI ECK-EN HAT MEIN HUT; UND HÄT' ER NICHT DREI ECKEN DANN WÄR' ER NICHT MEIN HUT

Over and over it sang its simple, lovely nonsense to me. Where was I?

I threw aside a blanket that somehow covered my face and sat bolt upright. The cold, grey light of dawn revealed the squalid bunk room and the muffled forms of the sleeping men. My mate lay beside me, his face dreadful in unconsciousness. On a table by the cook's bunk stood a little clock; and the old man whose hour for getting up it sounded lay there with his strange mad eyes fixed upon me.

Although everyone affirmed that the river at Lapataia was not to be crossed on foot it had, thanks to the unscrupulous friendship of Francisco, become immaterial to us whether or not the patrón granted us horses. And on horseback we were to go— that roguery was arranged, carefully planned and agreed upon between our friend and us. It may be that the assurance which this independent arrangement lent to our demeanor worked subtly upon the prejudices of our hosts, or that they were impressed by the mate's eloquence in praise of me; they wavered and then changed their minds.

"The señor is," I heard the mate telling them the day after our arrival, as I sat by feigned indifference, "a very great man, and much in the confidence of the President of the United States, of whom he is a close relation. He is also an intimate friend of the President of Chile."

And so he prated on until at last the patrones, after drawing apart for consultation, announced that we were to be taken on horseback across the river, and then left to

YENDEGAIA BAY

continue to Ushuaia as we pleased. "Very good," we said; and, it suiting their convenience, we set out again on the following morning, December third.

"Good-bye Francisco, good-bye poor, crack-brained cook, good-bye young Don
Antonio, and may the sweetness in you somehow flower despite the blighting meanness of the Croat soul." We splashed through the sparkling shallows of the bay; the
bright sun warmed us, the west wind swept the two days' dust of memory from our
spirits. God, it was beautiful to be released again and on our way!

Near the mouth of the bay we turned inland and rode for hours through the forest
on a beaten track and then, near noon, we reached the river. We laughed that they
had said we couldn't cross it! Not waist deep it flowed over a broad gravel bed
between firm banks.

Some distance beyond the ford at a turn of the winding river stood the buildings
of an abandoned lumber mill. Here we stopped for lunch. And here, after filling

(129)

our bellies to contentment, we parted from the friendly Chileño who had been our guide.

The trail to Ushuaia was well travelled and not difficult to follow. With our packs again upon our shoulders we set off blithely: ten miles it scaled on the map. Allowing, we thought, two more for devious winding of the way, we should get there—it being now one o'clock—by five.

We strode along through interminable miles of forest that revealed no glimpse beyond it but of high peaks and far descending wooded slopes. Finally, when the shut-in monotony most seemed to promise no relief of change, we came, to our astonishment, upon a railroad track, and, following this down the steep grade, emerged upon the shore of Beagle Channel.

Here in a field of the greenest grass that I had seen since leaving North America stood a little bright red cabin. It was strange thus to come at last upon that shore that had lived for me through Darwin's pages as a forbidding wilderness. And yet from that tiny verdant spot of cultivation we beheld across the channel the lofty mountains of Hoste Island, and its shores unchanged since ninety years ago the *Beagle's* men explored them.

The little cabin was untenanted, and since it appeared to promise that we were near to Ushuaia—just around the hill we thought!—I doffed my disreputable clothes and attired myself in the rather shabby "best suit" that my pack contained, adorning my flannel shirt with a necktie.

Nothing, of course, is more dispiriting than the postponement of what the heart is set upon, and no hearts can have yearned more poignantly for a fulfillment than ours—that weary last day of our journeying afoot—for the haven of Ushuaia. Not *one* hill did we round to bring the town to our view but twenty; and as we toiled on hours more with the hope that every hill and turn would be the last, to find ourselves again confronted with interminable pasture lands, disheartenment weighed like an added burden upon us.

There was not one trail but a thousand sheep-worn paths threading their aimless way between the clumps of califata; so even our immediate way was winding, and what the meandering miles of the shore added to the journey is only recorded by the too frequent milestones that our weariness bestowed.

We had almost despaired of reaching port that night, when, on attaining another "last" hilltop, we sighted far away the long peninsula of Ushuaia, a treeless golden neck of land lying, as it seemed, upon the blue surface of the bay. How then, with new courage, we hurried on to cross the many intervening miles before the darkness came is but a story of growing tiredness and frequent rests. We were footsore; and the mate's lameness that the two days' rest had profited now returned and pained him almost beyond endurance.

There still were many hills to climb and a deep stream to cross before, just as the finger shadows of the mountain peaks reached out to dim its glory, our eyes beheld the glistening roofs and towers of the town.

Westward of Ushuaia is a broad plain where once, a mile away, the English Mission stood. Twilight descended as we crossed it. The mate was spent with pain.

"Let's rest a bit," he said as we reached the outskirts of the town, "because we've got to blow in in style."

In a few minutes he could stand it. With heads thrown back and swinging arms, to our marching tune of "John Brown's Body" we tramped in.

The dogs announce our coming, folk come to their doors and stare.

"Where are you from?" asks a fellow.

"Admiralty Sound."

"God! Where are you going?"

"CAPE HORN!"

CHAPTER XVIII

USHUAIA

AT the head of a beautiful little bay that opens upon Beagle Channel, isolated by an almost impassable wilderness of mountains from all land communication with the world, stands the town of Ushuaia with its population of some hundreds or a thousand souls, the farthest southern "city" of the world. Overshadowing the town, by its organic importance in the life of the community if not by the vastness of its stone and concrete walls, stands the penitentiary; and from the barred windows of that prison a thousand men look out, during the months or years or lifetimes of their confinement, over the grey, cold, wind-swept waters of the south, or past a desolation of tin roofs and fire-devastated hills, at mountain barriers more terrible than prison walls. Yet the austerity of the visible world, far from imposing its gloom upon the inmates of the prison and the town, makes the security of their confinement and their small comforts appear as blessings wrung from the vast and pitiless desolation of the encompassing universe. Ushuaia, *because* of its isolation, is a cheerful, friendly place, where the townfolks' simple lives are just as full of gaiety as those of some great capital, and, one may venture, just as barren of real happiness; and where the care-free convicts walk the streets about their work in scarcely guarded freedom.

Into this town we two had tramped, ragged, dirty and tired, with all the goods we owned upon our backs and nothing in our pockets. And had the people, after staring and smiling at our grotesque appearance, decided to lock us up for mad it would have been less to wonder at than that on perceiving our madness they somehow caught its spirit from us. And when to all who questioned us as to our purpose we replied "Cape Horn," they answered "Crazy! but good for you!"

(132)

Most fortuitous of all was our immediate and open-hearted welcome into the house of Martin Lawrence, who, as the first citizen of the town, at once in point of time and wealth and the deserved high character he bore, by his friendship established our respectability in the public eye and opened the way to all that friendship and credit that was forthcoming to advance our purpose.

Yet still Cape Horn remained not only a purpose to which by our soul's desire and our outward boastfulness we stood committed, but a problem so difficult of solution that it occupied our minds to the exclusion of every other thought. That Ultima Thule of mariners is not, most readers must be told, the southermost point of the continent of South America, nor of Tierra del Fuego, nor even of some great island nearly adjacent to it. It is the southmost point of a small rocky island of a forlorn and isolated group, the Wollastons, and lies, scaled in a straight line, about seventy-five miles southeasterly from Ushuaia. We did not propose, having adventured thus far, to content ourselves with standing on the limit of the shore to gaze off seaward—and yet for that we were completely and exclusively equipped. Yet we could pace that long water front and look at the varied craft that lay at anchor in the harbor and discuss which one could serve our purpose best.

There was a tall-masted schooner of American build, a fine-lined vessel of that queenly type that is supreme in its class over everything that sails the seas: she was too big for us to dream of chartering. There was a smaller schooner, a clumsy, service-able craft: she was provisioning for a sailing voyage. And there was Lawrence's big sloop, the *Garibaldi*, but she was constantly employed in traffic on the coast. One other boat was there, a smaller sloop of about ten tons: she was of the very size we wanted, and she was idle. Upon somehow acquiring her we set our hearts. And that we might in our poverty as well have coveted the yacht of an emperor never, in our fatuous and unreflecting eagerness, occurred to us.

The owner of that much desired craft was one Fortunato Beban, a Croat, a prosper-ous and enterprising merchant of the place—as prosperity and enterprise were meas-ured there. In company with Martin Lawrence I sought him out. He was a tall, spare man of sixty-five, of forceful and distinguished appearance. His face was tanned and weather-beaten and from the shadow of his yachting cap his pale, blue eyes gleamed with the shrewdness of a New Englander. Beban heard my story and considered. Yes, he would rent the boat; the terms he'd have to think about. And although the inter-view had been friendly enough my heart sank.

We *had* to wait; and with the excuse that Beban's procrastinations afforded I re-signed myself to the enjoyment again of such delicious refinements of civilization as clean sheets and comfortable chairs and dainty food, and above all the society of the Lawrence household.

How pleasantly they live in Ushuaia! At evening we would stroll, my host and I, along the hilly streets up to the outskirts of the town and in the silence that the hour imposed, look over the broad bay and channel to the hills of Navarin and the white mountains of Hoste Island. Then at twilight, while the massed clouds hung still flaming over the darkening steel-blue mountain peaks, we'd enter some quiet, comfortable drinking place and sit conversing for an hour. And Lawrence opened up the past and told me something of his boyhood there in Ooshooia where, in years before the town was built, the flag of England waved above the little mission. He spoke without illusion for, born of missionary parents, the second white child of Tierra del Fuego, he knew the harsh privations of the early missionary's life and understood the sordid humbug of it. Yet his words recalled the fact that the savages had once in thousands peopled those shores that now, thanks chiefly to the pestilence of Christian mercy, were and would forever be a solitude.*

Those days of idleness, of waiting for that mind of Beban, ponderous with craft, to form its pronunciamento, brought me some memorable acquaintances. The house of Don Julio, the barber, whom I early sought, was one of the most attractive and pretentious in the town. It stood upon a little hill and overlooked the bay. I mounted the imposing stairway at the front and rang the bell. A little man of maybe fifty, pallid, sensitive, with large mournful eyes, opened the door—Don Julio. He greeted me with the sweetest courtesy, and, conversing in French, explained that he had been at work in his garden when the bell had rung. His house, in which he lived alone, was beautifully neat and revealed in the little conveniences for housekeeping of the owner's contrivance, in the hideous collection of pictures and souvenirs disposed so lovingly about, an active personal attachment to the place that made its ugliness delightful.

But his own bedroom was one of the world's great wonders. An ornate double bedstead, a miracle in lacquered brass, stood in the central space; an ancient counterpane of yellow satin, wrought in silk and gold with twining morning-glory vines, covered the bed. Over the lace-edged pillow slips were pinned embroidered satin shams, and shadowing these hung velvet curtains from a gilded canopy. Upon the flower-papered walls hung, pitching forward, gilt-framed colored pictures of the love and hate scenes from Italian opera. On stands and scroll-work bracket-shelves wonders of porcelain and painted shell rivalled the splendour of the festooned tidies that they

---

*A census of the Fuegian Indians compiled in 1883 by the Rev. Thomas Bridges, fifteen years after his establishment in Ushuaia as the first resident missionary, is as follows: Yahgans, 273 men, 314 women, 358 children; Onas, not more than 500; Alacaloofs, not more than 1,500; total Fugiana, about 3,000. Ten years earlier, he estimates, the number must have been double. It was a part of the missionary program to segregate the little Yahgan girls in what were called "Orphan Homes." The Orphan Home at Ushuaia was a small cabin. The children were packed eight in one room; the window was kept shut; there was no fire. Every day the inmates were taken for a walk, under guard. Mr. Bridges' report in 1883 for a period of three and a half years shows that 38 children were taken care of during that time. Of these, 18 are listed as having died of tuberculosis, 15 are not accounted for, 5 are recorded as living. The missionary remarks in his report that he experiences some difficulty in persuading the mothers to part with their children, as they fear that they will never see them again. Forty years have passed. Mr. Martin Lawrence, of Remilino, estimates the surviving Yahgan population at 60 souls. Mr. William Bridges allows the Onas 56 men and boys, 57 women and girls, 50 little children, 16 half-breeds.

TIN AND GRANITE

stood upon. A crimson-flowered carpet was on the floor, and crimson, gold-edged portieres darkened the still too garish daylight of the lace-curtained window.

"It's wonderful!" I whispered. And going to the window drew the lace aside and looked out at the world. It was blue daylight, hard and clear; over a few tin roofs stood the concrete walls of the prison; beyond this rose high into the sky the knife-edged mountain ranges.

Don Julio's bedchamber! I peeped into a tiny room or passageway just off the kitchen. There was a narrow iron cot neatly made up, one wooden chair with a shirt and trousers hung over it, nothing more. And here he slept.

Don Julio tied an apron around my neck, put the Barcarolle from "Tales of Hoffmann" on the phonograph, and cut my hair—beautifully. Then he poured me a glass of Benedictine and himself a drop of it for courtesy, proposed "Cape Horn—and back!" and we drank.

"Wait a moment, if you please," he said at parting—and ran into the garden.

He brought me a little bunch of forget-me-nots; and, with these quite foolishly in my hand, I strode out and down the street of the real world.

A town is but the home of men and women, and its spirit can only be read in the

MOUNT OLIVIA

lives of those that dwell there. Ushuaia is the resting place of a restless wanderer, Don Julio. His house is the treasury of his memories of the greater world he came from, of love and art, of pride and hope and failure. That state bedchamber is to him the symbol of the pomp he dreamed of and that might have been. Don Julio dusts its grandeur reverently, closes the door—and goes to weep upon his narrow, solitary bed.

Ushuaia is Fortunato Beban, hard and shrewd, making a little fortune for his heirs to spend. It is Martin Lawrence, cultured, intelligent and cautious—a stabilizer; Ushuaia is old Mr. Feeque who came there forty years ago to found the town.

This old man, a lean and feeble invalid, with the gentle face of one for whom the passion and activities of life are past, sits forever, deep in a tall-backed upholstered armchair, in a great room encumbered with a huge walnut double bed and a conglomeration of furniture, unwashed dishes, chamber pots, Catholic symbols, and lithograph portraits of the crucified Christ. Gently and very slowly the old man speaks, in cultured English; and his voice becomes at times so faint that one must sit at strained attention. And there is in his manner and appearance a beautiful and touching dignity, and in his speech the sadness of great wisdom.

(136)

I bore credentials which I offered him. "I do not need to see these," he said—and I was ashamed.

He loves his country, Tierra del Fuego, and has faith in its development; and he looks back upon past times of helpfulness to younger enterprisers in that land as on a life well spent in the service of a cause.

We drank coffee and cognac together. "Beban—" he shook his head. "Lundberg at Harberton," he counselled me, "is your man for the Horn: and if that fails get Indians and a canoe. It can be done that way if you must do it."

It being considered desirable by Mr. Feeque that I should pay my respects to the acting governor of the territory, I proceeded thither on the following morning in the conduct of Mr. Feeque's son. Whether the young man became conscious of my shabby appearance, or had mere natural tremors on approaching the great, when we had passed the outer sentries and were entering the vestibule he turned to me nervously and asked if I had my credentials with me. On being told that I had not he showed a sudden panic and a disposition to flee while there yet was time. But, not to be deterred, I drew him along with me; and a moment later we found ourselves seated in what is termed, I suppose, the audience chamber—a large crimson-carpeted room with ponderous hangings at the great windows.

The acting governor was a young man of pleasing manner who affected slightly and quite becomingly the indispensable inflation of his rank. Fortunately he was accompanied by a German secretary, by whose able interpretation we were enabled to converse fluently.

The art of conversation between persons of unequal rank is, of the whole histrionic art of conversation, the least difficult; and in direct ratio to the difference in rank it approaches the elemental facility of the burlesque, becoming in fact such a travesty in mock heroics as every mind must delight in as a release from the toil of sincere utterance. After an exchange of compliments, I proceeded at once to the business that weighed upon me. I sketched briefly the advantages that would be reaped by the Republic of Argentina from my published disclosures of the truly mild and equable nature of the climate of Tierra del Fuego; I hinted that American capital, freed from a deterrent dread of this maligned region, would stampede into a development of its resources; and I suggested as not impossible—and, though God forbid it, it isn't—that summer hotels for tourists would some day be erected among the Alpine splendours of these mountains.

"I would have asked you," I concluded, "to put at my disposal any battleship, cruiser, or transport that had been stationed here—had any been."

The governor replied—and with entire sincerity, I believe, so great is the courtesy of South Americans—that were any government vessel now in those waters it would certainly be placed at my service; and although he was at that moment powerless to be of assistance to me I might count upon him to do everything that lay within his authority to further my noble aims. "But," he added—and herein was evidence of the isolation of Ushuaia, "my government is very neglectful of us here. As an example, we were last winter seven months without communication with the north: during this time all government salaries remained unpaid; the prison and the town ran short of food supplies and tobacco, and, even worse than that—for it was a menace to the security of the people—the many convicts whose terms expired during those months were of necessity released upon the town without either money or means of support."

Thus ended my audience—to the satisfaction of all of us and the relief and pride of young Mr. Feeque, who had been profoundly impressed.

Beban, meanwhile, "considered"; and I waited. My mate lay on his back with a foot so swollen he could hardly stand on it; yet all the time his only worry was our problem of a boat. Lundberg, at Harberton, was forty miles away on Beagle Channel. We were growing desperate.

An old timer, who had searched the shores of all the islands to the south for gold, said one day, "I'll take you in a *dory* to the Horn."

"Good!" I cried with sudden hope.

He laughed. "Not on your life!" he said.

Despairing of getting a reply from Beban I had set a day to cross in a small boat of Feeque's to Navarin in search of Indians—it seemed the only thing to do—when, in the stillness of the early morning, I heard the chugging of a motor in the bay. A little sloop came in and tied up at the mole. And it was Lundberg!

CHAPTER XIX

KATHLEEN II

LUNDBERG came walking up the street. He was tall and lean and moved with nervous energy. Somehow, from far away, I knew the man and confidently hurried on to meet him. He was a Swede, forty, hollow-cheeked and tanned. His intent blue eyes showed the energy of his mind and its power of concentration. He spoke English fluently with an unusual and distinguished vocabulary. His pronunciation of words as they are spelt betrayed the self-educated man. Here was the pioneer who opens up new lands for human enterprise. Lundberg was a prospector, a lumberman, a business man, an organizer, a man of restless practical imagination. He knew the United States from Minnesota to California and Alaska, he had given years to a co-operative experiment in the jungles of Paraguay. His life had been one of fruitless accomplishment; and he stood now, at middle age, on the last frontier of the inhabited world, with nothing but a little five-ton boat, a timber concession, a devoted wife and four flaxen-haired children, good credit, and the respect of every man that knew him.

We had moved together to a public house and sat conversing over our drinks. "Well," he said after a long pause when I had finished my impassioned plea, "if you can get Beban's boat, do—and I'll stand credit for you. If you can't, I'll take you."

By a strange chance Lawrence came up at that moment seeking me.

"I have Beban's answer," he said with a sick grin. "Five hundred American dollars for the first ten days or less, and fifty dollars a day after that."

"That settles it," said Lundberg.

"And if we lose your boat," I said, as quickly as he had spoken, "I'll give you mine that's now in Admiralty Sound."

"If we lose mine," answered Lundberg solemnly, "no one of us will ever need another."

The only drawback to this fortunate solution of the problem of the means for getting to the Horn was that Lundberg was not prepared to start with us at once. His plans necessitated a delay of several days, and that, with my allotted time in South America drawing near its end, was exasperating enough. Yet could we have foreseen that the days of delay would on one pretext or another be lengthened to weeks we must at once with the discovery of his generosity have declined it. But, that being unknown, it was with wild elation that I returned to my bedridden mate and communicated the event to him.

It was with wild elation, too, that he weighed and got upon his feet, and in full sail of happiness bore out through the town. And that, "carrying on," he that day foundered over the deal table of a grog shop was at once to the credit of his consistent recklessness and almost the undoing of us both in that fold of respectability which had sheltered us.

It was both natural and proper that Lundberg, after an excursion for logs to Lapa-taia Bay, should desire to visit and say adieu to his family at Harberton before start-ing with us on that "suicidal" voyage southward. And, in order to see more of that country, to relieve the kind Lawrences of the burden of supporting us and of the mate's now somewhat discreditable presence there, and especially to keep very close to that skipper upon whose humor we were now depending, we prepared to accompany Lundberg.

The crew of Lundberg's sloop consisted of a Finn named Johanson, of whom, since my hasty impatience with him at another time resulted in his death, more will be said. Besides Johanson, Lundberg had with him on this trip an Argentine lumber-jack, a temperamentally worthless fellow, who had or had not, it was said, served a term for manslaughter. Both of them now appeared at the boat too drunk to be of any assistance in loading. At the moment of sailing the men were helped aboard: Johanson was stowed in the cabin, and the Argentine was propped up forward on deck against the mast where the fresh air might benefit him, and where he continued almost throughout the trip in utter silence and with an expression of forlorn and sullen dejection on his face.

Johanson was a far more entertaining drunkard. He was riotously talkative, wav-ing his arms about as he conversed passionately in a debased German. "Ja, ja, ja!" he cried at last in exasperation, mimicking the only answer I could make to his incoher-ence; "Warum sags't Du immer ja!" And the humor of that delighted him for hours.

It was unavoidable that Johanson, who sat at the companionway, should share occasionally in the potions of gulls' eggs and cagna (a raw white Argentine brandy) in which the rest of us indulged from time to time; but that besides this he visited a jug of wine, when he periodically crawled forward, we didn't discover until the

REMILINO

following day. Albeit he kept in the highest spirits, varying the diversion of conversation with now and then stopping the engine or climbing up on deck to struggle with the steersman, whichever one of us it might be, for the possession of the tiller. But each time we'd promptly push him down below—which he accepted in perfect good humor.

I had produced my flute and stood half out of the companionway playing it. At this Johanson pushed himself up beside me and stood with his broad good-natured face quite close to mine and stared at me with a curious solemnity.

"Many of us," he said after a long time, "can see beautiful things and want to make music; but we can't do anything about it. I would give anything in the world to play that flute."

Of Lundberg's boat more will be said at another and more impressive time. It is enough to say that on this rough day she sailed abominably and took more water on the deck than the *Kathleen* would have taken in a week. But there was intermittent power in the engine and, having left Ushuaia about noon, we entered the narrow passage north of Gable Island just as darkness closed about us.

To this point the shore of Beagle Channel had been mountainous with only in the vicinity of Remilino any land of comparative flatness. From Gable Island onward, however, both the island and the mainland were open rolling pasture land with sand banks fronting on the shore. These were the sheep lands of the Bridges' estancia, to the headquarters of which, at Harberton, we were bound.

It approached midnight when we were but midway through the narrow winding channel, and it was suggested by Lundberg and approved by all of us that we lie out the night at a camp on Gable Island that was at present being occupied by Mrs. Nielsen, the wife of the Harberton manager, and several of the children. Coming to anchor in a little cove we left the sloop in the hands of the two inebriates and them in the hands of God, and rowed to shore, where, above the low sky line of the land, loomed the dark shapes of a group of buildings.

We had landed and were approaching the most removed of the buildings, a little house that stood some distance up the hill, when we were hailed from the obscurity of the doorway by a boy's voice, as cheerfully as if no visitors could come, however late, unseasonably. It was but a minute later that I stood within the house at the doorway of a dark room and was presented by Lundberg to the invisible mistress of the place. And the sweet and girlish voice that greeted me out of the darkness is invested in my memory now with the aura of a mystic communication of that youthful happiness that was to irradiate the lives of all of us throughout the weeks that we were guests at Harberton.

CHAPTER XX

ARCADIA

IT was a blue day, a springlike, sunny, happy day, when we set sail with all of them on board for Harberton, and the gaiety of a holiday excursion attended our progress over the calm blue water. We stopped at a small hummock island and went ashore to gather gulls' eggs in the grass, scattering in every direction in the eager, laughing competition. Then with laden pails we embarked again. Soon the harbor mouth was reached, soon came the house into view; ah, it was good to reach that shore! And yet how vastly deeper now would my emotion be, how poignant as at the dearest home-coming, if destiny should ever lead me to that spot again!

For now at Harberton we entered on such happy weeks as might have held Odysseus longer than ten years from home. Yet about those unpretentious grounds and buildings there was little—beside the fair exception of the terraced flower garden—to suggest to the eye the comforts and the pleasures that we found there. The boxlike buildings in their garish red and yellow paint were plainly ugly save that they had the grace of fitness for the thing they were. The surrounding meadows and pastures had but the mild beauty of a cultivated rolling country. True, such quiet scenes possess a tranquillity which is a moral quality akin to beauty and that is perhaps more enduringly contenting to the spirit; yet, Harberton, even with the blue sea almost encircling it and lofty mountains bordering the inland plain, was in no way comparable to the prodigious splendours that characterize that southern land. One quality it did possess that next to the pervading spirit of the warm and joyous hearts it sheltered gave it character, that was tradition.

Harberton was the first practical and permanent result of English missionary activities among the Yahgan natives. Granted as a freehold to Thomas Bridges, the

(143)

THE GARDEN, HARBERTON

first and last superintendent of the mission at Ushuaia, it became for him an immediate stepping-stone from godliness to wealth. And, although his enterprising sons soon blazed their way across the mountains into the more fertile prairies of the north, the house at Harberton still displays in its plans and furnishings the Victorian middle-class comfort that dignified its golden days.

Through my stay at Harberton I came, by the observation of numerous memorials of the past that it contained, and by a reading of the tragedy that without words was written in the solitary love-bedecked grave that lay within a grove nearby, to have some understanding of the lives that had been spent in making it, and to have a little insight into the sorrow of loneliness that attends such isolation.

But all that sorrow appeared closed and ended with the musty past. It was written in the fading photographs of hard-handed sons of the frontier lugubriously posing in the imported attire of dandies against the background of the wilderness, in the faces of the sad-eyed women at their side, women that the wilderness had never bred, whom—all but their yearnings—it could only strangle. The tragedy that spoke in their forlorn pretentions to gentility was as the affliction of another world, as it was indeed of a generation gone. Today at Harberton was joyous with young life; and in the contemplation of that, in mingling with it and partaking of its spirit, one felt that here was the very abode of contentment, that here in reality in this last place was happiness.

My recollection of those weeks at Harberton is of days continually fair—fresh, sweet, cool, summer days when sitting on a hillside in the sun yielded the contentment of a fireside; and nights where in the serene inclosure of four walls the warm hearth and the astral bodies of ourselves became a solar cosmos more intimately friendly and no less vast than the cold immensity of out of doors.

My memory is of days on horseback, scouring the miles of rolling open pasture land, along shores heaped with the grass-grown mounds of shells that mark a thousand transient camps of vanished generations of the vanished Yahgans, on paths through the tall dark forest, across broad streams and inlets of the sea, following deep, thundering gorges of the river—to emerge at last into the peacefulness of some sheltered pond or lake—over and through this Paradise, day following day, we'd ride. Some days we'd picnic in the woods, choosing a sunlit clearing sheltered from the wind, and over a great fire we would roast a quartered sheep, and feed the crowd of happy children and ourselves; and then play children's games for hours on end.

The days went by like hours. On one pretext or another Lundberg put off sailing with us to the Horn until after Christmas. Meanwhile, to lay in stores and presents for the festival, we went on a trip to Ushuaia, my mate and I, with Lundberg and Johanson. Starting at noon we made Remilino at supper time and, being welcomed there, we stayed the night.

The pasture lands of Remilino are not comparable to those of Harberton and consequently that estancia, although nearly as old a foundation, is, while undoubtedly a very efficient, certainly a less pretentious establishment. It is a Lawrence freehold and is operated by the brothers of Martin, to whose generosity we were indebted. It was a privilege there to meet old Mr. Lawrence who with the Reverend Thomas Bridges had been one of the founders of the Anglican mission at Ushuaia in the year 1869. In the presence of this gentle old man, whose experience of the mission's failure, if it had brought some understanding of the futility of such a Christianizing enterprise, had in no way dimmed his simple Christian faith, one felt above one's condemnation of all murderous good intent a reverence for the kind, brave spirit that had burned in some of those blind saviors.

Then too at Remilino one could observe the effect that "civilization" had upon the natives. In a row of cabins that stood adjacent to the house lived several families of Yahgans who were employed on the farm. Yet the occupying of white men's shelters appeared to have effected little or no important change in the manner of their lives. They lived in their cabins as they had lived in their own wigwams. And even an elevation by marriage to the white man's state and rank, as was also to be met with there, seemed but the unkind uprooting of a spirit from that native soil from which it drank its happiness. We do believe, who have heard the notes of the wood thrush on some mountain side at evening, that in the music of the voice lies the soul's utterance. On rising in the morning at Remilino I stood a long time in the kitchen passage and listened to the low, sweet tones of the Yahgan women in laughing conversation at their work.

On arriving at Ushuaia that morning we went at once about our various commissions, I, for my part, making such purchases as I pleased on Lundberg's credit: before noon we were ready to sail. Johanson however, having received his wages, had browsed off somewhere and was not to be found. There was no doubt about the condition he would be in when we should locate him, so, after wasting half an hour's time in search, I impatiently urged Lundberg to leave him behind. This he reluctantly consented to do; and, tying up his effects, we deposited them at Lawrence's store. We were never again to see Johanson.

Of his end this is the story as it is known: after consuming his money in a grand debauch he set out on foot for Harberton to rejoin Lundberg there; he reached Remilino in shaky condition, a sick man. The following morning, still very groggy, he continued on his way. It was some days later when a man from Remilino passing through Harberton informed us of this. Johanson meanwhile had not appeared, and he was never heard of again.

There was no concern whatever about this disappearance of a man. He was no good, he was gone—and that was an end of it. My mate spent a day on horseback in search of him, but on that precipitous wild trail it was quite futile.

Meanwhile Christmas drawing near we were occupied with preparations for its

THE HOUSE AT HARBERTON

O du fröhliche,—
o du selige —

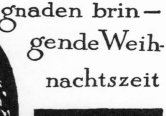
gnaden brin—
gende Weih-
nachtszeit

celebration. In the carpenter shop, behind locked doors, two of us were busily con-
triving gaudy wonders for the tree; gilded nuts, and cakes and candy wrapped in tin
foil saved from cigarettes, and tinsel made of shavings of sheet lead, and to crown all
a great star of Bethlehem with copper wire rays. The mate was set to dipping little
tallow candles and hanging them to cool. The children gathered daisies in the fields
and roses in the garden, and flowering boughs and mistletoe; they decked the house
as for a May-day festival. And on the last day the youngsters came trooping from the
forest with the tree, a glossy-leafed canelo, first of its kind that should attain the
glory of a candle-lighted Christmas martyrdom.

It is Christmas Eve and a great party is assembled at the Neilsen house. Besides the
Neilsens and Lundbergs with their eleven children, Bert Lawrence has come from
Remilino with two more children. There are in all eight grown-ups and thirteen
youngsters. Profound expectancy possesses them all, for the doors of the great state
dining room that is seldom used are locked upon a mystery, and the windows are
darkly curtained against the lingering daylight and the eager curiosity of little eyes.
Waiting, whispering, wondering at the doors, suddenly there is silence there as from
the closed room comes the sound of music—far away at first, and faint but heavenly
sweet. "Fröliche Nacht":—an orchestra is playing!

The great door swings slowly back and swells the sound into a burst of glory: but the light! the glistening, dazzling marvel of that tree revealed to eyes that never saw a Christmas tree before! Those that have done it feel the spirit of the children's happiness; and the rude music mounts to fervent utterance of their speechless wonderment. —Yet what an orchestra it was! two boys with fiddles, and the phonograph and flute—a band in tune with homemade tinsel and candles made of grocery string and tallow, but, like those homemade splendours, perfect there and then.

Then with eating and drinking, with dancing and laughter and play, the night glides by; and as the little children fall asleep weary with happiness, and the dusk of midnight brightens into dawn, we older people, mellowed by the wine and kept awake with happiness, contentedly converse into the rising day. The cock crows and the red sun rises through haze. We stroll into the garden and with the sweet air of early morning breathe the fragrance of the roses.

"Never," says Neilsen, "in the twenty-six years that I've been in this country have I known such a Christmas."

Lundberg's reasons for delay were without end; and their elusiveness somehow detracted nothing from their plausibility. Our sailing appeared now to hang upon the arrival of an Argentine transport, the *Rio Negro*, on which he was shipping logs to Buenos Ayres; but the date set for that ship's arrival vacillated tantalizingly over a period of weeks. Nevertheless, while cursing inwardly at fate, we made the most of the festivities of New Year's eve and of the Kingpin Punch that, out of an instructive resourcefulness bred of the suppression of home, I originated—to the vast credit of America and the second and almost fatal undoing of the mate.

KINGPIN PUNCH

Into a five-gallon kerosene tin, well scoured, of course, put all the raisins, prunes, currants, figs and stuff of that sort that you can find in the larder; add to this some hops, if you have any—just a few; ten pounds or so of sugar and a little sour dough—or yeast. Pour on hot water and mash. Fill with warm water and stand behind stove. In two days it will murmur gently, in four days it will growl. Abstain from tasting until the tenth day, which should be New Year's eve. Unleash and serve.

In the morning I discovered that the mate had not slept in his bed, and on coming down I found the family in a tragic mood over an occurrence of the night, of which I had known nothing. While the mate still slept where Neilsen in his wrath had hurled him, his case was tried. It hung on the decision whether or not his unconsciousness, as he lay in a heap where he had fallen at the door of a room that was not his own, was real or feigned. I knew the mate too well to have the slightest doubt and defended him as well as I was able on the plea of innocently bestial drunkenness; but the issue lay with him, and going to where he lay I wakened him, and to his emerging consciousness delivered my mind:

"You are no worse than an utter damned fool without a shred of character. Go down and talk to Mr. Neilsen, and either clear yourself with him or get out of the house and live on the boat."

Thanks chiefly to the understanding sympathy of Mrs. Neilsen, a reconciliation was effected and the mate continued, in diminished favor, under that hospitable roof.

To reinstate my discredited mate in the readers' hearts I shall narrate a brighter incident that occurred during these last days at Harberton and one in which his very countenance of brutishness shall delight the mind. For some weeks it had been rumored that a great steamer laden with sightseers was on its way from Buenos Ayres to tour the channels of Tierra del Fuego. And one day, lo and behold! the ship appeared off Harberton itself and anchored in the channel. Wild excitement reigned among us. Mr. Neilsen and Lundberg being absent from the house I was requested to do the honors of host to the multitudes that landed. There were hundreds: ponderous dowagers and gouty Argentine aristocrats, pretty girls and gay young gallants, jolly boys and solemn duffers, manicurists and hairdressers off for a lark, courtesans touring for pleasure and profit, and one elderly American scientist who looked with haughty contempt upon his shipmates. And certainly they were a silly lot, these white-gowned, dainty-slippered ladies and toy dandies now come to mince about that wilderness, and by the contrast of their alien grandeur turn its people's wealth into poverty and their contentment into hankering.

While Mrs. Neilsen and Mrs. Lundberg prepared the house for their reception I led the multitude up through the meadows to the hilltop, hoping that the quiet prospect there of rolling pasture land and sea would content them, yet always at a loss to think of any "wonders" to display to their impatient curiosity.

"But where are the Indians?" some cried. "Yes, show us the Indians!" echoed the crowd; and clamoring for Indians they thronged at my heels.

I felt by now a showman's responsibility and, as if I were somehow involved in a humbug, actually dreaded disillusioning my spectators. On one hope or another I led them on: the way grew thorny, fences obstructed it, too. Playfully screaming, tittering, protesting, they followed on a mile or two—and then my plan was formed. Eluding them I slipped through the underbrush and with all possible speed returned by a short cut to the house. There, near by, I found the mate in ardent conversation with a little blond lady. With the barest courtesy I drew him hastily away and into the house.

In the smithy stood a barrel of long horsehair; my oil paints were at hand; there were cats' skins in the storeroom and rags and ragged clothes; and above all artificial properties of savagery were the mate's own ugly, scarred and almost toothless face and his terrific chest and arms.

A quarter of an hour later a dreadful apparition crept out of the rear door of the house and walked across the adjacent pasture. At that moment the vanguard of the returning sightseers hove in view over the brow of the hill. Down they trooped,

FALLS NEAR HARBERTON

gayly chattering and laughing—when suddenly one stopped and pointed. All eyes followed the direction of that hand, a commotion swept over the multitude.

"Look! look!" they cried to me who then approached. "An Indian!"

"You are in luck," I said as I too discovered him, "for here, by the merest chance, you see the dreaded Yahgan Chief, Okokko, the most bloodthirsty of the race."

How I led the palpitating crowd nearer, nearer to that object of their curiosity and fear, how mothers called their daughters to beware, how gallant fellows quieted their trembling ladyloves, how at ten paces distant the boldest stopped while at their backs the others crowded close and formed a ring about the spectacle—all that is told. And there the savage sat, a fearsome object, naked to the waist but for the skins of wild animals that were rudely tied across his swarthy back and breast; while from the mass of coarse black hair that hung about his shoulders peered out a dusky face of such debased and sullen ferocity that nothing was left to be imagined of the abandoned brutality of that savage nature.

"A thoroughly bad character," I was saying to the crowd. "He is known to have killed and devoured three white men and a woman."

(151)

"But why are his arms tattooed?" asked an elderly woman who was regarding the beast through her lorgnette.

"It was done by a renegade sailor," I replied, my wits leaping into action, "who after throwing his lot in with these savages was at last treacherously murdered by them."

"Why he has blue eyes!" exclaimed a very pretty girl.

"Ah, there you have hit upon a very interesting story," I answered, sparring for time; and I spun a tale of an escaped convict from Ushuaia who had mated with a Yahgan, and through his own savage talents had become the leader of a tribe and the founder of a lineage of chiefs. And, as the mate grew restless under the continued scrutiny I hastily passed around my cap for a collection of money and cigarettes, which having completed I told the crowd that the savage showed signs of approaching anger—and was promptly rid of them.

"Just like an American!" said the Argentines later, while laughing over the trick that had been played them; and in this may be read what the world thinks of us.

But the joke was popular; and, binding my savage mate's hands behind him with a stout rope, we carried him aboard the steamer to horrify and delight the remaining hundreds there.

We have reached the eighth of January. While in almost hourly expectation of the steamer *Rio Negro's* arrival word came of another postponement, but this time with the definite assurance that she would be at Harberton and ready to load on the sixteenth. To put off our trip to the Horn until after that date was made out of the question by the urgent necessity of my own return to Punta Arenas; to go before then Lundberg refused—and without an engineer we couldn't run the boat. Suddenly it came to me, what I still believe to have been the truth, that Lundberg himself would never risk that trip. The situation was desperate.

Then a new plan occurred: to be carried to the nearest point of Navarin Island, to cross it on foot to Rio Douglas on the southwest shore, and there with an Indian and a canoe, as had been suggested by Mr. Feeque, make a dash for the Wollaston Islands. Lundberg readily consented to carry us across the channel, and the following day was set for the start.

That day dawned, beautiful with blue and gold, and all was ready for our crazy scheme—when, riding down the trail toward the house, appeared a horseman. All knew him at a glance—CHRISTOPHERSON!

In extenuation of the preceding omission from these pages of this great man's name it must be said that, although in Ushuaia and constantly by Lundberg we had been told of Christopherson as a mighty seal and otter hunter, as a mariner familiar with every rock and little anchorage of those waters—even to the farthest Wollaston Islands, and of all men the best fitted to get us somehow to the Horn, he was at the same time known to be absent hunting seal on Staten Island a hundred miles to the eastward; he was therefore dismissed from our calculations. And lo! here, as an angel of providence, he was!

Christopherson was a huge, calm man, a Swede. He spoke a broken English, softly, with a lazy drawl; he moved slowly, heavily; yet he was, somehow, the embodiment of latent energy and power. Moreover, he was familiar with Lundberg's boat and the operation of the engine, and he enjoyed her owner's unbounded confidence. To my proposition that he go with us in that boat to the Horn both he and Lundberg consented at once, with the proviso from Lundberg that she be returned to him before the sixteenth, as it was essential to his work of transporting logs for loading on the *Rio Negro*.

And so, with the morrow set for sailing, the days at Harberton had drawn to a close. Those many weeks of play and quiet occupation there in the comradeship of the two families had only deepened my sense that a great happiness was their lot as it had been mine while there among them. And my familiarity with the gentle landscape and the untroubled waters of Harberton had but awakened me to an appreciation of such quiet beauty as the true environment for contentment. I sat in the kitchen that last evening and told Mrs. Neilsen of what Harberton had meant to me, and that in the whole experience and travel of my life I had never known such happy lives as theirs nor lives whose happiness by the very conditions that bound them was so enduringly assured.

She had been busied about her work, but for some moments had not moved. I became conscious of the silence and looked up. She was crying.

"Oh, if you knew," she sobbed, "if you only knew what you were saying! You have been here so long—and yet you understand so little."

(153)

CHAPTER XXI

ALL ABOARD

LUNDBERG'S boat was sloop-rigged; she was narrow and deep; she sailed abominably. An old 20-horse-power Daimler engine was her chief reliance. This engine had lain for years under water; it was rusted and cracked, it was bound together with wire and plugged with putty and soap.

"The engine will never last to get there," said Lundberg. He spoke with gloomy conviction.

We loaded the boat with some ballast, put a spare anchor and a strong new chain on board, and sailed. And the farewells that were said were as solemn as at a lifetime's parting.

It was late at night and darkness came before we'd covered many miles. We anchored for two hours and sailed again at the break of dawn.

It was profoundly calm, and with a favoring tide we made Ushuaia just as the town was waking. Hastily I went ashore to purchase provisions and to comply with the formalities of the port; we were impatient to get off.

"Get six cases of gasoline and put them aboard," had been my parting instruction to the mate.

It did not occur to me that any misunderstanding could arise over so simple an order, and I put the matter comfortably out of my mind for the moment.

Ushuaia is not a busy place; for lack of occupation people lie abed. So that, whereas by now the sun stood high, folks still were lingering over their morning coffee, and the stores were shut.

It was almost two hours before I could procure my purchases, and get my dispatch

Sierra del Fuego

Ushuaia Bay

BEAGLE CHANNEL

Remolino

Harberton

Cable I.

Cape Mitchel

Murray Narrows

Button Island

Woollya

Dumas Pen.

Ponsonby Sd.

Rio Douglas Mission

Navarin Island

Picton

Banner Cove, on Picton I., marked with a cross, was the scene of the suffering that led to the death of Capt. Allen Gardiner

Lennox I.

Pasteur Peninsula

Wickham Bay

Guanaco

TEKENICA BAY

Tekenica Mission

Eclipse Sd.

Gardner Bay

Packsaddle I.

Packsaddle Bay

Lennox I. was the scene of the gold rush of the nineties Gold is still found in the beaches of this coast.

Hardy Peninsula

NASSAU BAY

Gaston Island

Orange Bay

Bourchier Bay

Grey I.

Grafton Bay

Beaufort Bay

South Bay

Deep Bay

On Bayle I. was established the first mission station It was soon moved to Tekinica.

Wollaston

False Cape Horn

FRANKLIN SOUND

Freycinet I.

Map—
Showing our course from Harberton west- ward to Ushuaia, south- ward to the Wollaston Islands, and return to Harberton January 1923.

Hermit I.

Herschel I.

Deceit I.

Hall I.

Horn I.

CAPE HORN

PACKSADDLE ISLAND

from the sub-prefect.* At the end of that time I hailed the mate to take me back aboard.

"Oh," says the mate as I step into the skiff, "about the gasoline: they could only let me have five cases."

"Well, that's aboard, isn't it?"

"Why no; we thought we'd better wait to see you about it."

And there, by that stupidity that meant half an hour's more delay, was sown the seed that bore its bitter fruit in the tragedy of disappointment that was to follow.

It was still utterly calm when we weighed anchor, and calm as we passed into the bay. At the point of Ushuaia Peninsula a light breeze met us from the westward and broke the mirrored landscape of the channel. The wind increased. Half an hour from

---

*ROL.—de la tripulación de la lancha Nacional *Ellen* matricula 25309 y de 5/70 toneladas de registro, zarpa el lastre con destino a cabo de Hornos.

———————————————————— ROL ————————————————————

Patrón...........................Ernesto Christopherson.......................................Sueco
Marinero ....Ole Ytterock.......................................Norte Americano
Mayordomo ....Rockwell Kent................................... "   "

Ushuaia, Enero 11, 1923

MOLINO,

Ayudante.

sailing we were in mid-channel. It blew a gale and the seas broke over us; we made no headway. Coming about, we ran for the shelter of a group of islands off the peninsula and anchored in their lee.

The wind increased and raged all afternoon and evening. We were held all night at that anchorage, and the lost half hour became twelve.

At two in the morning we awoke. It was cloudy and dark and calm. Not for an hour would the wretched engine start; then, in the grey dawn, we crossed the channel to the lee of Navarin, skirted its shore among innumerable islands and, entering Murray Narrows, headed south. It began to rain.

The passage between Navarin and Hoste Islands is in places very narrow; the shores are steep with many jutting headlands but not mountainous. They are clothed in forest. It was a gloomy wilderness and dark, that early morning in the rain, and the successive landmarks of missionary disaster were vested with a gloom fitting to the tragic spirit of their chronicles.*

Leaving the southeast point of Dumas Peninsula we entered upon the crossing of Ponsonby Sound. There was not a breath of wind and the snow-topped mountains of Hoste Island that stood as islands above the hanging banks of cloud were reflected in the grey mirror of the sea. In an hour we had crossed the sound and were entering on a long winding passage that transcepted the nose of Pasteur Peninsula. The shores were low and sparsely wooded with a ragged growth of dwarfed and tortured trees. In the tall grass of a little clearing stood a native settlement of three or four dilapidated shanties and two wigwams. No sign of life was there and we passed on.

Presently we turned abruptly into a very narrow channel, an uncharted passage with which Christopherson was familiar, and after proceeding for some miles as if upon an inland river, emerged quite unexpectedly into Courselle Bay near the southern extremity of the peninsula. Here were cream-colored rock cliffs of an unusual formation with tufts of brush-grass whiskering their faces. At their base were deep passages and caves, and these were alive with hair seal.

---

*In 1851 England was horrified by the news from Tierra del Fuego of the death through starvation of Captain Allen Gardiner and his little missionary band and crew. The record of their fears and sufferings remains in the astonishing diary of the captain that was found "miraculously" preserved beside his bones; and the reader of it is torn between admiration of a religious devotion far more wonderful than that of Job, and disgust at its driveling foolishness. However, to the martyrdom of Captain Gardiner, "sailor and saint" as he is naïvely called in a memoir of his life, was reared a monument—the South American Mission; and in the extermination of the Yahgan race through the Mission's benevolence the death of the captain may be said to have been most completely avenged.

Keppel Island, one of the west Falklands, was made the station from which, by means of a schooner—named *Allen Gardiner*, missionaries might communicate with Tierra del Fuego, and to which natives might be brought for instruction. The first steps toward a rapprochement with the Indians were facilitated by the re-discovery of Jemmy Button, who, as readers of Darwin's "Voyage of the *Beagle*" will recall, had been taken when a child to England, educated there, exhibited before the Queen, and then returned to his own people. Jemmy Button, now grown to middle age, still kept alive that spark of English speech which the divine breath of missionary zeal might fan into the flames of the redemption of his race.

So it was brought to pass that Fuegian boys were taken back to Keppel; and if most of the children died during the years of their instruction, it was at least a solace that they died redeemed. Poor little Peter Duncan—once named Multgliunjer! He was only eleven when death carried him away. "I loved little Peter Duncan," writes the missionary home, "he was obedient and kind. I shall sorely miss him; as I look

PASTEUR PENINSULA

ANCHORAGE OFF BAILEY ISLAND

Experience had taught us to distrust fair weather; and, with hope so strongly set upon our destination, we never entered upon a passage of open water without anxiety lest a wind should rise and retard us or drive us back to shelter. But the day held always calm—the hushed unnatural and portentous calm of forces mustering for a storm. We crossed Tekenica Bay and passed between Packsaddle Island and the mainland of Hardy Peninsula; and then, with only rain clouds darkening and ob-

around the school-room I shall not meet with his bright smile, nor remark the beauty of his eyes again. Poor little Peter! He was accustomed to say, 'I want to be like Jesus!' "

It happened that the *Allen Gardiner* was carrying back to their home on Navarin two little fellow Indians of Peter. Now it was not the tradition of those savage people to respect property—they merely loved it. The two lads saw aboard the cutter many little things they liked, and they had opportunity on the long voyage from the Falklands to attach a few of these. They did. The articles were missed, the boys were searched, the lost was found. The captain was a stern and upright man, and he reproved the boys accordingly and called them names, no doubt, that little Christians early learned the horrid and disgraceful import of.

It was Sunday when the *Allen Gardiner* anchored at Woollya, and, while the boys—hotly resentful of the captain's anger—

mingled with their relatives on shore, the captain, accompanied by his entire crew—excepting the cook, who was in the galley busied with plum-duff—proceeded to one of the native wigwams, where he began the solemnization of divine service.

The Yahgans were unusually interested this Sunday morning; they gathered about the Christians in a great crowd. And when the benediction had been said they took up sticks and stones and killed the white men one and all.

The cook, hearing the uproar and discovering its cause, jumped overboard and swam ashore. He fled into the forest and eventually, in miserable plight, reached the south coast of Navarin, where he fell in with another tribe of natives. These, there being nothing to be gained by killing him, treated him well; and after a lapse of time he was picked up by a ship and returned to his own land.

POACHERS' CABIN, BAILEY ISLAND

scuring the horizon, headed across Nassau Bay for the northern point of Grévy Island.

The low nearer shores of the Wollaston group were visible, but only occasional cloud rifts faintly disclosed the mountain ranges of the farther island. And finally, as we neared the point of Grévy Island it rained, obscuring everything but the very shore we skirted. It was, therefore, not the anticipated wilderness of rocks and mountains that greeted us but islands mildly desolate in character with treeless plains of yellow grass fringed at the shore with green. However, as we penetrated Gretton Bay, the mountains loomed out through their veils of cloud and showed the grandeur of the region we had entered.

CHAPTER XXII

AN ORGY AND A CHRISTENING

THE Wollaston Islands are the last group of the archipelago of far south-western South America, the last peaks of the descending Cordillera to emerge above the sea. The western trade winds, checked and diverted by the mountain ranges to the north, sweep with accumulated violence around their southern end and make the Wollastons a region of prevailing storms. Their high peaks comb the clouds for those last miseries of hail and snow that heaven can inflict on desolation. No one inhabits them.

We were therefore startled when, on entering Victoria Channel where we intended lying for the night, we saw smoke ascending from a supposedly untenanted camp on Bailey Island that in years past had been Christopherson's. A long low shanty built of boards and tin stood on the shore with the luxuriant green bank of thicket at its back. A rod or two away, partly concealed in a grove of canelo trees, was a tent-shaped Indian wigwam.

As we approached, a rude skiff manned by two men put out from the shore and pulled to meet us. Pausing near us as we anchored, but keeping a few yards of water between the boats, they looked us over with obvious curiosity and distrust. Whatever might have been their fears of us, their own appearance was far from prepossessing. They were an unkempt, dirty-looking pair, a white man and an Indian. The white man was young and, in spite of a scraggly growth of silken whiskers, rakishly handsome, yet with the meanly pitiless eyes that are often the accompaniment of effeminate beauty. Bringing his scrutiny to some conclusion, he greeted us, invited us to come ashore, and then rowed back.

Taking along two bottles of fiery cana and a quarter of mutton, we landed and

SOUTHWESTWARD FROM THE SUMMIT OF BAILEY

went up to the house. We entered a dark and filthy interior that revealed its furnishings only when our eyes had become accustomed to the gloom. The room was long and narrow; on a box opposite the door stood a small rusty cook stove; there was a stool and two or three kerosene tins to sit on—but no table; a chest, some bags of provisions, and, on the floor, two mattresses in opposite dark corners. From the rafters hung some half-devoured kelp-geese, dripping gore; a great pile of mussels and shells was heaped against the wall—and in the ooze from these a brood of goslings puddled. Here in this squalid filth lived two families; we were introduced:

Vasquez—the man who had greeted us, a murderer—free after a term at Ushuaia.

Genevieve—a pleasant, pretty, brown-skinned, dark-eyed, slatternly young Argentina *fille de joie*—his wife.

García—a male, aged fifty, a creature in no definite way deformed yet of as hideously forbidding an aspect as one might ever meet. He was short and pot-bellied; his huge-calved legs curved backwards as with out-turned toes he postured like an uncouth dancing master. His brow retreated; it was bald and lofty, and his hair waved from its apex like the plume of Hector's helmet. His large grey eyes—blond eyes with yellow whites—were set in protruding heavy-lidded sockets; he rolled

WESTWARD FROM THE SUMMIT

them about as though disdainful to disturb the ponderous repose of his huge head. The great moustache of a dragoon half hid a coarsely sensuous mouth and veiled in shadow the pitiful retreating chin. Barefooted in the muck of the floor this being stood, hands clasped Napoleon-wise behind, his chin pressed into the wrinkled hide of his neck, and, with the ferocious dignity of an imbecile, silently regarding nothing—García, ex-inspector at the prison of Ushuaia.

Margarita, his wife—a Yahgan of perhaps twenty, pathetically gentle, sweet and servile—and her child not more than three months old.

And Berté, the Yahgan—he looked forty, said he was sixty, and proved it by accounting for twelve years at an English mission. The Yahgans are not beautiful. An accurate observer in the year 1884 describes them: faces "flat, wide, round, and full; cheek bones prominent, forehead low and wide on line with eyes; nose flat; eyes very small and without lashes; lips swollen and hanging; strong jaws and good teeth. Very small hands and feet, thin arms and crooked legs." Berté was of stocky build and seemed a powerful fellow. He lived alone in his wigwam, a very decent, tidy place.

These people were subjects of Argentina, hunting otter on the soil of Chile; they were poachers living in fear of detection and the law.

And now on one of the most remote and desolate spots upon the earth we stand in this dark and squalid den, confronted by as villainous a crew as ever fought for pirate treasure. We are unarmed. Night is descending.

The murderer is pouring out cana; he advances toward me bearing two cups, and hands me one.

"Señor," he says, "they tell me that you are an artist. I consider artists, writers and musicians to be the greatest people in the world. I drink to your prosperity: salud!" And, with the most candid, charming smile, he touches my cup with his, and we drink.

"Victor Hugo and Tolstoi!" he continues, "they are my favorite authors. What greatness! what grandeur of conception!"

And, as we proceed to discuss the extensive literature of Europe with which he is familiar, Genevieve, our graceful hostess, pours out more cana. "Salud! Salud!" The den's a festive hall this night by candlelight, a friendly, riotously jolly place. "O Genevieve, sweet Genevieve," I sing, entrancing her. Vasquez is charmed, Margarita smiles as she suckles her babe, the inspector rolls his eyes at me and sternly nods.

Vasquez throws off his coat and dances—wild, disgusting, beautiful by the sinuous grace of his lithe body. Margarita laughs and Genevieve screams with enraptured merriment. And they shudder playfully when Vasquez, with the long, keen bread-knife in his hand, enacts for us the drama of his murder.

And Berté dances, sodden with drink, some still-remembered war dance of his race; and then relapses into the sullen lethargy that we had roused him from. The drunken

THE INSPECTOR

primitive! He sits there with his head dropped on his breast, a long time, silent; then suddenly he raises it and bawls out one shuddering obscenity—at which the women turn away and hold their ears; and their eyes laugh.

Margarita sits there silently, her maternity in affecting contrast to the drunken uproar. "Are you happy here?" I ask her, seating myself at her side. She speaks a little English, murmuringly, in a low sweet voice.

"No—not happy," she replies, modestly concealing the breast which her child suckles.

"Do you like it in Ushuaia?"

"Yes."

I look from her drooping moon-round face, as calm as Buddha's, from her sad and gentle face, to that sullen brute, her mate. She is watching me.

"Do you love him?" I ask.

Her face is hidden from me when at last she answers very quietly, "Yes—I love him."

On being asked the name of her child, Margarita told me with distress that it had not been baptized and that it bore no name. It was a girl. I don't know what possessed me then—but in a spirit far removed from levity, although I have no faith, I told the mother that I would perform the baptism and give the child the name of my wife. The father was brought into consultation, and, on being assured that I was qualified to carry out the ceremony, entered into the plan with serious interest. My mate did his part with unexpected dignity, explaining in Spanish to those present the nature of the ceremony and directing the conversion of the den into a chapel. The floor was somewhat cleared of its litter and in the center was placed a kerosene tin as a support to the font. Genevieve scoured out their only basin, a great thing of pink enamel, and, filling it with rain water, placed it on the tin. Behind the font I took my station with the babe in my arms and its parents on either side; the others stood in a group facing us a little way removed. At a sign of my hand all became reverently silent.

"Dear God:" I prayed, "may this little child thrive in health and beauty and somehow out of the misery of its birth emerge into happiness; and in token of this prayer I baptize and christen her in the name of God, Kathleen Kent García." And I touched her brow with water and kissed her.

"In what church?" asked García when I had finished.

"There is but one God," I answered.

"El mismo Dios!" they repeated, in moved tones.

Being asked for a certificate of baptism I composed one and gave it to García, with a letter to old Mr. Lawrence begging him not to repudiate my act.

How we got aboard that night no one could recall. We awoke in bright daylight. The wind was blowing with the velocity of a gale, making it difficult even in our comparatively sheltered anchorage to row to land. Wind-bound, we spent the day ashore and, to accommodate Christopherson, took the entertaining Vasquez for a walk. He was in high spirits and vauntingly told me that the ceremony of the pre-

HORN ISLAND

ceding night had pleased him particularly as it was in truth the baptism of his child. So much the better for little Kathleen, I thought.

On this day the dreary bog lands of Bailey Island lay golden in the sunlight, while the many ponds that were dispersed about the plain mirrored the deep blue of the zenith.* The stunted trees confined to the depressions of the land were evidence of the prevailing force of the wind.

*A mission was established on Bailey Island in 1877 with a Mr. B— in charge. A few years later it was moved to Teke-nika. B—'s reports are amusingly free-and-easy documents that stridently bemoan the looseness of the native morals which permitted little girls of eight to marry married men. "I shall make them lead better lives," he said. So he put the girls into an Orphan Home and undertook their instruction with such ardour that it became the scandal of Fuegia. B—'s carryings-on came to the knowledge of Mrs. B—, and upset her terribly; it reached the ears of the bishop clear over in the Falkland Islands. It was too much. Official action was resolved upon—when suddenly, in the very nick of time, Mr. B— fell overboard and was drowned. It was beautifully reported in the missionary magazine at home: "One day, from causes which have not been ascertained, Mr. B— was drowned by the upsetting of his boat in the bay, to the inexpressible sorrow of his wife and children. Too late the sad event was noticed on the shore; but it shows the devotion and courage of the native women, who were first apprised of the occurrence, that they plunged into the surf and swam toward the spot, in the hope of saving their friend, although the tide was high and again and again they were thrown back by the waves. But although Mr. B— passed from the scene of his self-sacrificing labours, the effect of his teaching remained, and bore fruit among the natives." There is an epilogue: some time later a skull was picked up on the beach and acclaimed as Mr. B—'s. It was carefully placed in a box and put in the chapel, pending shipment to the Falklands. An Indian boy, one Cyril Mäteen, was among those sent to fetch it. He took Mr. B—'s head out of the box, held it up before him, and with a broad grin apostrophised it thus: "O you white man! you like love my countrywoman."

The following day still holding us wind-bound, I set out with the mate for the summit of the island, a mountain eleven hundred feet in altitude. The way lay over inland flats of bog and marsh, and stony hillsides, and through thickets of matted brush and wind-dwarfed trees. The day was one of alternating sun and rain. After our first cold drenching we learned to watch the squalls approach and seek in time the shelter of a rock, or make a refuge of boughs piled on the top of a low-branching tree. Under such shelters we would huddle, shivering with cold, and let the rain drive past us on the gale.

After a last steep ascent of several hundred feet we reached the mountain top, and, clinging there against the storm, beheld the vast and fearful wonder of the region of Cape Horn. Through the drifting murk of the clouds appeared a wilderness of mountain peaks with the torn sea gleaming at their base, stark islands with the storm's night over them or glistening with a sunshaft on their streaming sides, or veiled illusively in falling rain. And, as we looked, suddenly the darkness of a midnight closed around us, obliterating everything but the pinnacle of rock on which we crouched for shelter.

Then the squall struck—and the screaming fury of it shook our faith in the stability of granite mountain peaks. White lines of hail streaked past, hiding the universe in their perpetual stream. The world became to us that bit of rock we clung to, a cast-off meteor fragment hurled through space.

And then, as suddenly as it had come, the squall had passed; and we were back again upon a mountain peak. But it was winter now, and the sun shone on slopes white with new-fallen snow.

Our eyes turned southward. The jagged range of Hermit Island was shrouded in a passing storm. Hall Island off its eastern end was almost lost in the obscurity of vapors that engulfed the south.

"Look!" we cried.

The vapors parted: past the hard, dark edge of Wollaston appeared a cloven point of rock, faint and far off, with white surf gleaming at its foot; Horn Island!

We have seen it! And the vapors close.

CHAPTER XXIII

THE RAINBOW'S END

BERTÉ, sick from the debauch, lay in his wigwam. When we had called on him and asked his prophecy of coming weather the oracle had replied unfailingly, "Very bad." And so it proved. It was the fourteenth of January, the eve of the last day that we might keep the boat. The wind raged unabated, and it rained. It was unutterably dismal in that place. On board the boat the rain leaked through the hatch coverings and dripped on everything; and yet in seeking refuge on shore we were thrown in with the sickening debauchery and intrigue of that household. It was in truth the last place. And if in the world that we have travelled the possession of some property in luxuries and comforts had but bred in men a restlessness for more, here where there were none even the putrefaction stank with the ferment of discontent.

I stood looking out of the shanty and saw a change come over out of doors. The rain had almost ceased. I went out and walked to the water's edge. It was near sundown and the clouds had made it almost dark. But now a golden light transfused the atmosphere; and presently as I stood looking northeasterly across the water there appeared a rainbow faintly glowing there. Its omen of the pot of gold came to my mind and I remembered the gleaming arch that had spanned our southward way four months ago and that again had seemed to lead us through the mountains: and now, ever eluding an attainment, it beckoned northward! There is no rainbow's end, I thought. Yet even as I watched it now it grew more bright and more defined; a full arch blazed across the north, and its ends, passing the horizon, came nearer, approaching each other in the lower hemicycle. Now they were upon the very waters of the harbor and moved still calmly downward through the wind-blown spray like destiny

BERTÉ'S WIGWAM

THE SHORE OF BAILEY ISLAND

approaching consummation. The flaming circle closed: . . . . God! where the two ends meet was I!

Berté, as I approached his wigwam, came staggering out. At my anxious question about the morrow's weather—on which hung our last hope of attaining the Horn— he enjoyed a more than customary nonchalance in answering; he wasn't thinking about it, he didn't have to think; he knew.

"Tomorrow," he said at last, "not so bad."

We sailed at the first sign of dawn. Berté and the intrepid Vasquez unexpectedly appeared alongside in their skiff and asked to be carried through Washington Channel. We took them on board and the skiff in tow. In that dark canal between the mountains of Wollaston and Bailey Islands it was hushed and calm, so that our passage desecrated the silence, and the echo of the noisy motor flaunted, too soon, its puny arrogance at the slumbering Titans. Near the channel's southern end we met the ground swell's warning of the seas awaiting us outside, and from the mountain faces the awaking wind beat down in angry flaws. Then, entering Franklin Sound, we lost the last shelter of the land and were exposed to the unbroken force of the sea and wind.

SITE OF THE BAILEY MISSION

Close to the shore, in the lee of a small peninsula of Wollaston Island, we stopped to disembark our passengers. It was safe enough: they had the wind and the sea astern to make the bay. But their courage failed them and they fairly cringed with lack of resolution.

"Come on!" we cried impatiently, "get out!"

Somehow they clambered into the skiff. They had brought two guns on board: someone held the gun out to Vasquez, who seemed to grasp it in his trembling hands.

"Have you got it?" was asked. "Good!"

And the gun, released, slipped through his fingers and sank to the bottom of the sea. We tossed the rifle into the skiff, ordered them to let go—and bore away, leaving them frantically pulling for the shore. And now the Horn!

It was still the twilight of early morning—a gloomy twilight, for not a streak of crimson had broken the dark pall of the clouds. The crested sea was mountain high and tragically black, a restless tossing sea, not wind-blown but more terrible in that it seemed to lift and fall by some energy within itself. Our boat was slow in answering the helm; she was sluggish and dispirited and had no buoyancy to ride the crests but, like an over-laden tired thing, let them break over her and pour the length of her and weigh her down. It was raining, and we were drenched.

(175)

The companionway was a cramped shelter for three men. I went below and crawled on all fours through the dripping, smoke-filled, suffocating darkness of the hold to reach the forward hatch. If it happened to be fastened, it occurred to me, I'd never live to reach the air again. It wasn't. I propped it open—only an inch or two for breath; but a moment later a sea boarded us and poured a deluge through.

We had almost reached the middle of Franklin Sound. A strong wind had increased the sea's violence; we were being roughly handled and were making very little progress. The mate, holding the tiller, watched the seas with concentration so intense that his face had an expression of agony. Christopherson was as impassive as ever but not smiling. If my own countenance showed anything but painfully affected nonchalance it must have been faith—not faith in God but in Christopherson and Ole Ytterock, the mate. For a long time in the wild uproar of the engine and the sea and wind no one had spoken. Then Christopherson spoke in Swedish to the mate, and the mate answered—without taking his eyes from the water. Christopherson turned to me.

"I tank," he says quietly, "we must turn back."

"Can't we make it?" I ask.

"I tank not." And the mate looked at me and shook his head.

CHAPTER XXIV

VIVE VALEQUE

LATER and now in looking back upon that moment in Franklin Sound when we attained our "farthest South" I am inclined to forget how cold and miserable we were, and how hopelessly our little craft struggled to advance through those dark, huge seas; I belittle the terrors of the moment and reproach myself with having abandoned too easily, on the counsel of others, that last attempt to achieve what I had come so far to do. And yet fate timed with dramatic precision one incident that should make me calmly certain that our continuance against Christopherson's judgment would have brought failure and possibly disaster upon us. We had scarcely regained the shelter of Washington Channel when our motor failed; not for five hours would it run again.*

Besides the immediate necessity of returning the boat to Lundberg was that of my own return to Punta Arenas. The Steamship *Toluma* in which my passage home had been booked was due there, with some uncertainty, on the last of January, and, with much to attend to before leaving, it was important that I reach Punta Arenas as much in advance of that date as possible. My return journey bore the complexion of a race with time.

After repairing the motor we ran for Harberton—not by the sheltered route that we had come, but straight for the passage between Navarin and Lenox Islands. Very soon after leaving the Wollastons we ran into fair weather; and all day as we sped along with favoring wind under a sunny sky those forlorn islands appeared unchangingly shrouded in storm clouds.

*A recent communication informs me that two days after the motor brought us safely back to Harberton it breathed its very last.

ONA WIGWAM

We reached Harberton that evening: and it was a palliation for our abandonment of the Horn that the *Rio Negro* arrived promptly on the following morning: our sacrifice had not been unnecessary.

We had not, as it may appear, entirely forgotten that we owned a five-ton sloop, the *Kathleen*, of New York, still anchored in the remote waters of Admiralty Sound. On my description of her she was purchased, f.o.b. Punta Arenas, by Mr. Neilsen, and the mate was dispatched to rejoin her. Since I was not to see him again until six months later in Vermont I shall bring his story to a hasty conclusion. Proceeding on horseback as far as the cabin of Francisco in the valley of Lapataia—a journey of four days—he recrossed to Bahia Blanca, making the return journey through the valley, lightly burdened, in two days. There he found the scene of the mill changed by disaster. A hurricane from the southeast had completely demolished the main building of the mill. It had at the same time driven all the little craft at that anchorage ashore. The *Kathleen* fortunately was undamaged.

While waiting to be towed to Punta Arenas, as was to be arranged by me, the mate reconditioned her; so that on her arrival two weeks later at Punta Arenas she appeared as bright and new as on the fateful day that we had left.

Here the mate abandoned the agreement that he had made to return to Harberton to go into the service of Lundberg. Needing money, he accepted, with characteristic recklessness, the published challenge to all comers of the local pugilistic celebrity; and, after careful training and grooming as the white hope of the foreigners of Punta Arenas, submitted gloriously to an inglorious beating and a knockout in three rounds. Thus ended his immediate South American adventures.

And here we dismiss him. That in his life he will continue to "carry on" there is no doubt; but if he carries *through*, fortune must favor him beyond the merits of his purblind rashness.

From the affection with which I have written of Harberton must be judged my sorrow at what was to be perhaps a lifetime's parting from those friends. As if to make my memory of that happiness imperishable, it was a fair, sweet sunlit morning when I rode away; and my last far-backward view along the trail was of the gleam of waving handkerchiefs. Farewell, dear Harberton.

My route lay across the mountains to the head of Lago Fognano; from thence to the eastern coast to the estancia of Via Monte at Rio Fuego, northward as far as San Sebastiene and westward to Useless Bay. I had planned to continue to Porvenir and from there cross the Strait of Magellan to Punta Arenas by the boat that was in regular communication between those ports; but fortune, as will be told, shortened my land journey.

One of the Harberton men had been detailed to accompany me to the lake, and for my second day's long ride to Rio Fuego we led a spare horse. The trail was difficult, traversing miles of forest and broad stretches of bog where the dilapidated corduroy

ON THE INLAND TRACK FROM HARBERTON

was of questionable value under foot. It crossed the mountains at a high altitude, somewhat above the timber line and then plunged precipitately toward the inland plain of the lake. The trail on the northern side was particularly hazardous by reason of the sodden bog; and, then, as a warning of what might happen to the reckless horseman, we passed a horse with the brand of the Argentine constabulary mired and dead at the side of the trail.

Rain came with the twilight and we were yet miles from the Ona Indian encampment on the lake where we intended to stay the night. At last, tired and wet, we reached it, a scattered settlement of cabins and wigwams standing in a clearing somewhat elevated above the lake. We were hospitably received by the most prosperous resident of the place and invited into his cabin. There, seated on the floor beside the stove, were two women, one his wife—a woman of middle age—and the other possibly his daughter. And in that company I passed as foolishly embarrassed a first half hour as any in my life. While they stared at me with persistent amused curiosity at every word I uttered in an attempt at conversation they went into convulsions of laughter. I relieved the situation by producing the flute, and by its means transformed their ridicule into wonder.

The Onas as I saw them appeared a superb race. What dignity they must have pos-

PASTURES OF VIA MONTE

sessed in their savage state can only be guessed; yet even the disfigurement of civilized rags detracted little from the entire tall, lithe, free-limbed, straight-featured beauty of the young woman.

It happened on the following day that an Indian, one Nana, was going to Rio Fuego and I attached myself to him for guidance. The distance was upwards of sixty miles and an early start would have been desirable. Nana, however, delayed until almost noon, and then abruptly mounted and rode off without regard to me. However, I was soon upon his heels, although my horse, being heavy-burdened and somewhat tired from the journey of the day before, kept up with difficulty. For two hours Nana rode madly on, vouchsafing not a word to me nor even turning in his saddle to see how I contrived to follow. But finally he thawed, accepting cigarettes and food.

All day and into the darkness we rode across those rolling sheep lands. It was at last near midnight; for an hour a strange, far distant roar had reached my ears. A dense mist had settled over the land so that I lost all sense of where we were. We began the ascent of a hill. Suddenly, as I reached the top, the sound swelled to the cumulative magnitude of prolonged and never ending thunder, while below us, gleaming in the night, appeared the long white line of breakers on the ocean shore.

(181)

LAGO FOGNANO!

An hour later we reached the estancia of Via Monte, where, leaving my luggage with the Indian, I went to bed.

"Tell me something desperate about the Indian, Nana," I said next day to someone on the farm. "I need some book material."

"No need of inventing anything about that fellow," was the answer. "He's the strongest and most desperate of the lot—but they can't get the goods on him. He's known to be a horse thief, but they can't catch him at it. Last year he was married to a woman and her daughter and the daughter disappeared. They're sure he killed her —but can't prove it."

Here, though with the bravest will to shoulder my pack and tramp on through the wilderness to Porvenir, I found myself, at Via Monte, suddenly upon the very threshold of cultivation where, thanks to the friendliness of the British ranchers all along the way, to good roads and to Henry Ford, I found myself at the end of my pedestrian wanderings, and in six days, by the grace of encountering a steamer at Useless Bay, on time in Punta Arenas.

And now, having brought my Voyaging to a conclusion, I may, as at the church's benediction, turn with my little congregation toward that rainbow land of the far south and repeat my homage to its hospitality.

The Magellan Times
January 21, 1923.

Since the very day of my coming, I have found in Punta Arenas, in Tierra del Fuego, and wherever I have met mankind, such friendliness that I am moved to tender publicly my profound thanks for the generous hospitality of the land.

Tierra del Fuego! You tear yourself from the despairing embrace of weeping wife and children at home and come here over seven thousand miles of sea to show the world by combat with the elements, with cold and ice and with murderous savages, the magnificent valor of your manhood. What wild extravagance of fancy! Instead of bravery you are challenged in this wilderness to display the utmost of what decency and manners you possess that you may meet with due courtesy the kindness of even such blood-curdling, otter-poaching desperados as were our hosts in the Wollaston Islands.

We have had varied experience in our travels. We have seen the wilderness at its worst, and have travelled for days over country that no white man had ever crossed; and we have found that the worst is not too bad to be a pleasure ground for anyone who loves the wilderness enough to strap a pack upon his back and enter it.

And even the disaster that threatened us almost within the first hour we sailed seemed blessedly contrived that we might experience the hospitality of Dawson Island, of Marcou and of the Morrisons.

And we have seen the best. We've been at Lago Fognano with Robert Mulach, at Bahia Blanca with Don Antonio and Curly, at Ushuaia and Remilino with the Lawrences; and we have lived for weeks in that paradise which is called Harberton, where roses grow as big as sunflowers and where sheep don't get the scab. And if I live to be one hundred and fifty (as I no doubt shall) my memory of Christmas there with that dozen of happy children of the Neilsens' and the Lundbergs' will never fade.

I have crossed the mountains from Harberton to Lago Fognano, and seen there Ona maidens so ravishingly beautiful that one must marvel how I ever parted from them. I have ridden all day and

(183)

far into the night over the green meadowlands of the Kingdom of Via Monte and still not reached their end. I've started afoot with a heavy pack upon my shoulders from Rio Fuego to Useless Bay, and what with the Goodalls, and Jacksons, and Munros and Ross's, and Donaldsons, and Thompsons, been so helped along and housed and fed and put to bed in princely bedchambers that I may boast of having walked across the Island without ever touching foot to ground.

The pampas are profoundly impressive in their monotonous immensity, the mountains are at once a glory and a horror, an inert embodiment of overwhelming force. The forests are luxuriantly green, with stately trees, and violets starring their dark floors; and in them live the gentlest of wild creatures. It is a peaceful and friendly wilderness, neither intemperately hot nor cold. And everywhere among the settlers poor or rich the traveller meets a warmer hospitality, more trust, more generosity than he'd find elsewhere in a lifetime.

The
END

(184)